# ONE MORE SATURDAY NIGHT

# ONE MORE SATURDAY NIGHT

Reflections with the Grateful Dead,
Dead Family, and Dead Heads

BY
SANDY TROY

ST. MARTIN'S PRESS/NEW YORK

The Publisher wishes to express its thanks to all the individuals who have cooperated in making this book possible. Every effort has been made to reach copyright owners or their representatives. The Publisher will be pleased to correct omissions or mistakes in future additions.

Permission to reproduce printed text from the following sources is gratefully acknowledged:

THE SOUNDMAN SOUNDS OFF: AN INTERVIEW WITH DAN HEALY by Sandy Troy
Copyright © 1978 Relix Magazine, Inc., Relix Magazine, P.O. Box 94, Brooklyn, N.Y. 11229. All rights reserved. Used by permission.

THE RELIX INTERVIEW: BRENT MYDLAND by Sandy Troy
Copyright © 1980 Relix Magazine, Inc., Relix Magazine, P.O. Box 94 Brooklyn, N.Y. 11229. All rights reserved. Used by permission.

BALLAD OF A THIN MAN by Bob Dylan
Copyright © 1965 by Warner Bros. Inc. All rights reserved. Used by permission.

With the exception of the illustration on page 103 and the poster on page 180 all illustrations reproduced in this book are the registered copyright © of Stanley Mouse. All rights reserved. Used by permission.

The poster reproduced on page 180 is the registered copyright © of Family Dog Productions. Family Dog Productions is the d.b.a. of Chester L. Helms, 771 Bush Street, San Francisco, California 94108. All rights reserved. Used by permission.

BOOK DESIGN AND PRODUCTION BY ROCHELLE BRADFORD
TYPOGRAPHY BY TYPELINK, INC.

Library of Congress Cataloging-in-Publication Data
Troy, Sandy.
   One More Saturday Night: Reflections with the Grateful
Dead, Dead Family, and Dead Heads / by Sandy Troy.
     p.   cm.
   ISBN 0-312-05938-8
   1. Grateful Dead (Musical group) 2. Rock musicians — United
States — Interviews. 3. Rock music fans — United States —
Interviews. I. title.
ML421.G72T7   1991
782.42166 ' 092 ' 2 — dc20
[B]

                                         90-22497
                                              CIP


First Edition-May 1991

10   9   8   7   6   5   4   3   2   1

6/21

TO MY LOVING WIFE DEBRA
WHO WAS ALWAYS THERE AND
WHO NEVER SAID NEVER

# ACKNOWLEDGMENTS

This book is the culmination of my spending over twenty years enjoying Grateful Dead concerts. It could not have been written without the encouragement and support of the many Dead Head friends I have known. Special thanks is given to Dick Latvala, Eileen Law, Bob Menke, Rob Bertrando, Gary Frankel, Fred Harris, Jerry Moore, Pat Lee, Michael Johann, Barry Glassberg, Steve Benavidez, Peter Doft, Ron Ellner, Steve Young, Phil Galloway, David Etra, and Mark Harris.

For their cooperation in providing me with a lively and informative interview, I am deeply indebted to Jerry Garcia, Dan Healy, Phil Lesh, and Ramrod.

I am no less grateful to Nicki Scully, Carolyn Garcia, Rock Scully, Tom Constanten, Chet Helms, John Dawson, Tony Serra, Michael Hinton, Alec Levy, Gabe Harris, Steve Cornell, and Howard Betts, whose insights were invaluable.

I am particularly thankful to Stanley Mouse, who generously contributed his time and talent to this project.

Gratitude is given to the staffs of *Relix* and *The Golden Road* for so aptly documenting the history of the band over the years. I am also indebted to the folks at *DeadBase* for compiling the tour and set lists, which proved to be an invaluable resource tool.

I wish to thank Jim Marshall, Gene Anthony, Herb Greene, Michael Zagaris, Jay Blakesburg, Ron Delany, Brian Gold, and Tim Mosenfelder for making their extensive photo collections available to me.

For giving me the benefit of his knowledge and insight, I want to thank Professor Stephen Potts of the University of California at San Diego.

I am especially grateful to my agent, Tony Secunda, who had faith in me and helped me put this book together.

For their tireless efforts on my behalf, I want to express my unending gratitude to Rochelle Bradford, Betty Buckner, and my editor, Ed Stackler.

To Mark and Joanne Fenichel, thanks for the hospitality.

**Finally, to Brent Mydland, thanks for being a friend and playing a tune to make us all happy.**

# TABLE OF CONTENTS

nized the potential of the local music scene. Helms joined the Family Dog and began to organize dance concerts at the Fillmore Auditorium, and then at the Avalon Ballroom. Helms, who at one time had been a student at the University of Texas at Austin, brought to San Francisco a young blues singer from Texas named Janis Joplin, who eventually joined the band he was managing at the time, Big Brother and the Holding Company.

TONY MAGUIRE

JIM MARSHALL

**Chet Helms**

**Janis Joplin**

Another important figure in the burgeoning San Francisco music scene was Bill Graham, who in 1965 had been the manager of the San Francisco Mime Troupe. The Mime Troupe, as street theater, was frequently getting busted by the police, and Graham had to organize benefit concerts to raise bail and defense money.

A turning point in the San Francisco music scene came about with the success of the Trips Festival which was conceived by Stewart Brand, one of the Pranksters and later the originator of the *Whole Earth Catalogue*. In January 1966, Chet Helms, Ken Kesey and Bill Graham were all involved with putting on the Trips Festival at Longshoremen's Hall. Kesey brought the Pranksters and the Grateful Dead, Chet Helms brought Big Brother, and Bill Graham managed the business end of things. The festival lasted three days and resembled Kesey's Acid Tests, with multi-media light shows, live music, the Merry Pranksters, and LSD.

GENE ANTHONY

**Bill Graham**

**The Trips Festival**

The Trips Festival inspired Bill Graham to book his own concerts at the Fillmore Auditorium. For a short time Graham and Chet Helms shared the bookings at the Fillmore Auditorium, but Helms soon took his Family Dog concerts to the Avalon Ballroom.

Beginning with the concerts in early 1966 at the Fillmore Auditorium, and then also at the Avalon Ballroom, psychedelic posters were used to publicize upcoming concerts. Each concert had its own distinctive poster. Artists like Stanley Mouse, Alton Kelley, Rick Griffin, Victor Moscoso, and Wes Wilson made significant contributions to the posters for the Family Dog and Bill Graham concerts.

**The Poster Artists: Griffin, Moscoso, Kelley, Wilson & Mouse**

By the end of 1966, the Hollywood-based record companies had taken notice of the San Francisco music scene. The Jefferson Airplane, the Grateful Dead, and Big Brother and the Holding Company had all signed record contracts, with Quicksilver Messenger Service the last to sign at the end of 1967.

Allen Ginsberg at the 'Be-In'

The 'Human Be-In'

Aware of the increasing recognition outside the Bay Area since the January 1966 Trips Festival, counterculture organizers planned a larger follow-up for January 1967, called the "Human Be-In" to be staged in Golden Gate Park in San Francisco. It was a "Gathering of the Tribes," Berkeley political activists and hippies who had one thing in common — opposing the "Establishment." The radicals and the hippies had different agendas: One wanted to change the nation and the world, the other wanted to change your head. The Human Be-In, held on January 14, 1967, featured music by the Grateful Dead and the Jefferson Airplane, chanting by Allen Ginsberg and Gary Snyder, two Beat poets turned Eastern mystics who merged politics with head trips, acid guru Timothy Leary, and Jerry Rubin, leader of the Berkeley Vietnam Day Committee and future Yippie leader.

After the Human Be-In, the San Francisco counterculture began getting more national attention, but it was still largely a local phenomenon, as were the local San Francisco bands. Since most of the groups played songs longer than the two- to three-minute format required by AM radio, the main route to public exposure was closed. In April of 1967, a DJ named Tom Donahue, feeling that the music needed its own radio station, took over an eight-to-midnight slot on station KMPX-FM, initiating on so-called "underground" radio the very first FM rock program format, and featuring cuts from albums rather than singles. Similar stations soon started popping up in other parts of the country. At first record company executives sneered, but even they had to take notice of the audience swing in that direction.

The event that marked the Bay Area's ascendance as the mecca of the counterculture came in June of 1967 with the Monterey Pop Festival. The Monterey Pop Festival introduced the San Francisco sound to the mass media, giving the Jefferson Airplane, the Grateful Dead, Quicksilver Messenger Service, and Big Brother and the Holding Company their first exposure to a wide audience.

arlier that month, on June 2, 1967, the Beatles released *Sgt. Pepper's Lonely Heart's Club Band* in America, an album that pushed rock music beyond traditional instrumentation, and introduced myriad musical forms. With the release of *Sgt. Pepper's*, there is little dispute that the Beatles had put out the single most important album in rock music history. For a large part of the listening audience, it marked their introduction to psychedelic rock music. The Beatles' first project after retiring from touring, *Sgt. Pepper's* was a concept album and a unified work of art. It was also the first album to publish lyrics, indicating that lyrics were worthy of consideration. This made it a staple for FM underground radio, where an entire album side could be played without interruption. *Sgt. Pepper's Lonely Heart's Club Band* became the musical soundtrack for the "Summer of Love," and the unofficial anthem for the growing counterculture, which had developed an anti-war, anti-materialistic, spiritual philosophy.

Along with the Beatles, Bob Dylan also had a major influence on the style and substance of the '60s. Starting out as a folksinger, Dylan had written protest songs like "Blowin' in the Wind" and "The Times They Are A-Changin'," which challenged the establishment, espoused an anti-war philosophy, and advocated civil rights. When Dylan traded in his acoustic guitar for an electric guitar, he blended a folk message with a rock and roll beat and became the spokesman for his generation. A line from his song "Ballad of a Thin Man" was seized upon by media commentators when reflecting upon the counterculture: "There's something happening here and you don't know what it is, do you, Mr. Jones?"

In its customary way, the mainstream press tried to figure it all out. *Time* magazine devoted to the hippie movement its July 5, 1967 cover story entitled "The Hippies: Anatomy of a Sub-Culture." The Summer of Love had officially begun. Haight-Ashbury soon saw an invasion of people from across the nation. In the summer of 1967, about 50,000 young people migrated to Haight-Ashbury.

**JG & MG at the Monterey Pop Festival**

GENE ANTHONY

Haight-Ashbury surrounded the Panhandle of Golden Gate Park, and was not far from San Francisco State University, where many of the early philosophers of the hippie counterculture got their intellectual start. Hippie philosophy had a few basic premises. "Do your own thing" was a romantic notion of absolute freedom without restraints, which encouraged spontaneity, a sort of existential living from one moment to the next. Doing your own thing meant wearing your hair long if you were male, or going bra-less if you were female, or not shaving anything if you were either. Dressing up in colorful and creative clothing was common. Popular items were bell-bottom jeans, granny dresses, Indian feathers and headbands, paisley and tie-dye shirts, fringed buckskin jackets and boots, beads and bells, sandals and bare feet. "Peace and love" was the hippies' notion of a perfect world. Bumper stickers with the slogan "Make love, not war" started appearing on automobiles, and peace symbols started appearing everywhere. The notion of "the free trip" took root. Free clinics and other places for free legal advice, food, counseling, or a place to crash for a night were set up. The best-known support group was the Diggers. Led by Emmett Grogan, the Diggers would collect enough food each day to make a huge pot of stew, which they would dish out free in the park. They also had a free clothing stop where people would toss what they didn't want and pick up what they did. The Grateful Dead, Jefferson Airplane, Quicksilver Messenger Service, and Big Brother performed numerous free concerts in the Panhandle.

Not everyone shared the "do your own thing" philosophy, and on October 2, 1967 the Grateful Dead house at 710 Ashbury Street was raided by narcotics officers who arrested Bob Weir, Pigpen, their two managers Rock Scully and Danny Rifkin, equipment man Bob Matthews, and some friends that happened to be there. At a press conference that followed their release from jail, a statement prepared by Rock Scully and Danny Rifkin was read:

JIM MARSHALL

**Danny & Rock**

During the raid the police also confiscated files belonging to the Haight-Ashbury Legal Organization, which had offices in the Grateful Dead house at 710. Nothing significant became of the charges and the onerous law making possession of marijuana a felony was eventually changed to an infraction for possession of less than an ounce.

The Jefferson Airplane

Quicksilver Messenger Service

Country Joe

In keeping with the community spirit of Haight-Ashbury, the Grateful Dead, Jefferson Airplane, and Quicksilver Messenger Service pooled their resources and opened up the Carousel Ballroom on Market Street in San Francisco. The Carousel Ballroom, located in what had once been an Irish dance hall, was a beautiful old building with wooden floors, glass mirrors, chandeliers, and old tables and chairs. The official opening was on Valentine's Day, February 14, 1968, featuring the Grateful Dead and Country Joe and the Fish, and was broadcast on FM radio. Though there was always good music to be heard at the Carousel, after several months of losing money on shows, the Carousel was closed down, and was taken over by Bill Graham, who renamed it the Fillmore West.

Haight Street, March 3, 1968

With the influx of people into Haight-Ashbury, the atmosphere began to change. Not only had young people moved there in droves, but Haight-Ashbury became a tourist attraction. The Grateful Dead house at 710 Ashbury became a stop on the Gray Line bus tour. By March of 1968 Haight Street was getting so crowded with people that the city started closing portions of the street to vehicular traffic on weekends. On Sunday, March 3, 1968, the Grateful Dead, in a spontaneous gesture of goodwill to the Haight-Ashbury community, decided to give a free concert on Haight Street. Masterminded by manager Rock Scully, the band lined up two flatbed trucks back to back, which they used as a stage, and played in front of the Straight Theatre for a couple of hours to an audience numbering in the thousands.

By the end of 1968 the scene had changed so dramatically that many of the public figures of Haight-Ashbury migrated north over the Golden Gate Bridge to Marin and Sonoma counties. As a result of the exodus of musicians, artists, and merchants from Haight-Ashbury, the Summer of Love came to an end, but the influence of its counterculture lived on. With the rise to national prominence of the local San Francisco bands, the seeds of the counterculture that were planted in Haight-Ashbury were dispersed across the nation.

The Woodstock Music and Arts Festival confirmed that the seeds of the counterculture had indeed taken root and blossomed full-bloom. From August 15-17, 1969 nearly 500,000 people joined together for one wild and joyous weekend that helped define a generation. Ostensibly a rock concert, it became

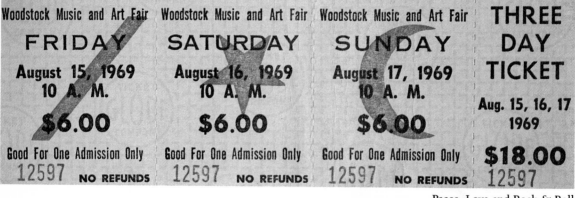

Peace, Love and Rock & Roll

**The Bus at Woodstock**

much more, a milestone in rock history that clearly showed our nation that the flowering of America had taken place. With the whole world watching, never had a hippie gathering been so large or so successful. Wavy Gravy and the Hog Farm commune helped run security, and the Pranksters drove "The Bus" out from the west coast and set up a free kitchen, gave first-aid, and helped kids who were on bum trips. Grooving to the music of more than twenty bands, the Woodstock Festival was a clear victory for peace, love and rock and roll. The performers included Joan Baez, the Band, Blood, Sweat and Tears, the Paul Butterfield Blues Band, Canned Heat, Joe Cocker, Country Joe and the Fish, Creedence Clearwater Revival, Crosby, Stills, Nash and Young, the Grateful Dead, Arlo Guthrie, Tim Hardin, Keef Hartley, Richie Havens, Jimi Hendrix, the Incredible String Band, the Jefferson Airplane, Janis Joplin, Melanie, Mountain, Quill, Santana, John Sebastian, Sha-Na-Na, Ravi Shankar, Sly and the Family Stone, Bert Sommer, Sweetwater, Ten Years After, the Who, and Johnny Winter.

However, it wasn't just the groups that made Woodstock so remarkable; it was the half million people who showed up and made it work. People supported one another, shared things, and became part of the performance. Billed as three days of peace and music, it became much more, a great Dionysian communal tribal experience.

As the euphoria of Woodstock began to fade at the end of the '60s, the early '70s saw the demise of most of the original San Francisco psychedelic bands. The Grateful Dead proved to be true survivors, however, persevering through a roller-coaster ride of ups and downs. Suffering managerial difficulties that caused them severe financial problems, the Dead went into the studio and produced two of their finest albums. The albums *Workingman's Dead* and *American Beauty* contain a selection of original songs that draw from the blues, folk, and country traditions of American music. The lyrics to most of the songs on both albums were written by lyricist Robert Hunter, a longtime friend of Jerry Garcia. During the early '60s in Palo Alto, Garcia and Hunter began playing folk songs together in a number of folk and bluegrass bands. Eventually the pair started writing their own tunes, collaborating on Grateful Dead songs ever since.

The Grateful Dead were able to improve their harmony arrangements on *Workingman's Dead* and *American Beauty*, with some help from their friend David Crosby, an original member of the Byrds. Crosby, who by then was a member of Crosby, Stills, Nash, and Young, had been hanging out at the Dead's ranch in Novato, California, jamming with various members of the band

Robert Hunter

David Crosby

**The NRPS at the Fillmore West, 1971**

and teaching them harmony. The listening public was obviously impressed with the sound of *Workingman's Dead* and *American Beauty*, which were well received and sold better than any of the Dead's earlier albums. Released in 1970 at a time when bands like the Byrds and the Flying Burrito Brothers had made country-rock music very popular, both albums proved to be big favorites on college campuses from coast to coast. In 1970 the Dead played almost 150 live shows throughout the United States. In the spring of 1970 the Dead started touring with The New Riders of the Purple Sage, a spinoff band that played country-rock music. John "Marmaduke" Dawson was the moving force behind the New Riders, a band which at that time consisted of Dawson on rhythm guitar, David Nelson on lead guitar, Jerry Garcia on pedal steel guitar, Phil Lesh on bass, and Mickey Hart on drums. It was at this time that "An Evening with the Grateful Dead" came into being, a format that included three sets of music: a New Riders set, an acoustic Dead set featuring many of the tunes from *Workingman's Dead* and *American Beauty*, and then a lengthy electric Dead set.

With the untimely death of Janis Joplin in October of 1970, and the breakup of the Jefferson Airplane and Quicksilver Messenger Service, it fell upon the Grateful Dead to carry on the psychedelic tradition of the '60s. More by default than design, the Grateful Dead were thrust into the position of being representatives of the '60s to a generation of high school kids and college students who wanted to be part of the Woodstock nation. By the early '70s elements of the counterculture had been absorbed into the American mainstream. Long hair and beards were commonplace and the recreational use of marijuana and psychedelic drugs spread to all sectors of American life. To a large segment of American youth, the Grateful Dead came to symbolize what the counterculture was all about.

While the Grateful Dead may have become representatives of the counterculture to a society in a state of transition, the band itself was in a state of transition as well. After drummer Mickey Hart joined the band in September of 1967, he added a new dimension to the music of the Grateful Dead. As much a percussionist as a drummer, Hart's energy and creativity transformed the Grateful Dead from a dance band into an ensemble that stretched the boundaries of rock music. The band became a septet with the addition of Tom Constanten in November of 1968. Constanten, a close friend of Phil Lesh, was a classically trained pianist with experimental leanings, and he added yet another dimension to the overall sound of the group. The Grateful Dead, as a septet, were capable of an extraordinary level of interplay between improvisational melody lines and rhythms. The album *Live Dead*, primarily recorded at the Fillmore West at the run of shows on February 27-28, and March 1-2, 1969, captures the Dead at the height of their improvisational ability. The septet lasted little more than a year, as Constanten left in early 1970 to pursue other musical interests. The Dead were able to make the transition quite smoothly, however, due in part to the shift in direction the band had already been taking with the music on the albums *Workingman's Dead* and *American Beauty*, and to the increase in popularity the albums brought them.

David Crosby, who had helped forge the sound of *Workingman's Dead* and *American Beauty*, was joined by several members of the Dead who jammed with him at the Matrix in San Francisco in December of 1970, performing some of Crosby's classic songs. Garcia, Lesh, Kreutzmann, and Hart, had been helping Crosby on his solo album *If I Could Only Remember My Name*. Garcia also contributed to the Crosby, Stills, Nash and Young album *Deja Vu* by playing pedal steel guitar on "Teach Your Children."

Throughout 1971 the Grateful Dead's popularity steadily increased. In typical '60s style the Dead participated in an ESP experiment at their show at the Capitol Theatre in Portchester, New York, on February 18, 1971. Mickey Hart, who had an interest in parapsychology, arranged with Dr. Stanley Krippner of the Maimonides Hospital Dream Research Laboratory in Brooklyn, New York, to have a psychic subject in a dream state at the same time the Grateful Dead asked the audience at the Capitol Theatre to concentrate on a series of six slides projected on a large screen behind the band. The object of the experiment was to see if the audience could project any of the images on the slides to the psychic under controlled conditions. The test proved a success when the subject closely identified four out of the six slides. The show also proved to be a turning point for the Dead since Mickey Hart decided to leave the band. With the departure of Mickey Hart, the band had to further simplify the arrangements of many of their songs.

Europe '72

The closing of Bill Graham's Fillmore East and West marked the end of an era. The Dead's last shows at the Fillmore East included guest appearances by Duane Allman, the Beach Boys, and Tom Constanten. At the Dead's last show at the Fillmore West the band made a dedication to their longtime friend Owsley. When the Fillmore West closed its doors for the last time on July 4, 1971, it ushered in an era of bigger venues.

By the fall of 1971 Pigpen's years of excessive drinking were taking their toll and he was unable to tour for health reasons. The Dead brought in Keith Godchaux to play keyboards. Godchaux debuted on the fall tour at the University of Minnesota on October 19, 1971. His wife, Donna Jean, also joined as a vocalist a few months later. In December 1971, Pigpen returned after a period of recuperation, and then toured Europe with the band in 1972. The band and an entourage of Grateful Dead family rolled across the continent in a pair of buses for nearly two months, playing over twenty concerts. One bus was designated the "Bozo Bus," while the other one was called the "Bolo Bus." In typical Prankster tradition the band donned bozo masks and performed that way to several unsuspecting European audiences. The Europe '72 tour turned out to be Pigpen's last tour and the last time he sang with the band in public. Though Pigpen did play keyboard one last time at the Hollywood Bowl in June of 1972, Europe was his last hurrah.

Bobby Ace &
Donna Jean Godchaux

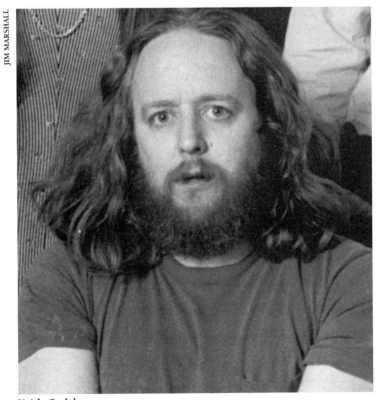

Keith Godchaux

The Dead traveled to Veneta, Oregon, in August of 1972, to perform at a benefit for the Springfield Creamery, which was owned by Chuck Kesey, Ken Kesey's brother. On a hot summer day the Dead performed on a field with a stage erected at one end to a crowd of approximately 25,000 people. In such a beautiful outdoor setting, the magic of the '60s was recaptured on that sunny afternoon. In splendid '60s style, people danced with reckless abandon, and when clothing became optional due to the oppressive heat, smiling faces became the password of the day.

**Dead Heads Dancin' in the Sun**

While 1973 marked another year of transition for the Dead with the loss of Pigpen, who passed away on March 8, 1973 after a long and debilitating illness, it was also a year of immense popularity for the band. Touring extensively, they played a number of outdoor shows during the spring and summer in order to cope with the increased size of their crowds. On May 26, 1973, along with the New Riders and Waylon Jennings, the Dead played Kezar Stadium, an old football stadium right in the midst of the Haight-Ashbury district. A joyous crowd danced in the sun and reveled in a celebration apropos of the legendary Haight-Ashbury. Traveling to the East Coast, the Dead then played to sold-out audiences at RFK Stadium in Washington, D.C. on June 9-10, 1973. The Allman Brothers were also on the bill, and on the second night at the close of the show a jam session involving members of both bands ensued. On July 28, 1973 the Grateful Dead, the Allman Brothers, and the Band played at a "summer jam" at Watkins Glen, New York, to an estimated crowd of more than 600,000. Larger than Woodstock, the "jam" had attracted the largest gathering of rock and roll fans in history. A few days later the Band also shared the bill with the Dead for two sold-out shows at Roosevelt Stadium in New Jersey on July 31, and August 1, 1973, helping to make Jerry Garcia's birthday on August 1 a real party.

Roosevelt Stadium, August 1, 1973

The Grateful Dead formed their own record label in 1973 so that they could handle all aspects of the record business themselves. Grateful Dead Records was established to produce Dead albums, and Round Records, a subsidiary of Grateful Dead Records, was formed to accommodate the band members' solo projects. The Dead's attempt at independence from corporate America went beyond records, however, and by the end of 1973 they had set up their own travel agency, Fly By Night Travel, handled extensive mailings to a vast number of Dead Heads, and designed their own elaborate sound system.

A Beardless Garcia in Front of the 'Wall of Sound,' Hollywood Bowl, July 21, 1974

Playing larger and larger venues, stadium shows became common, and the sound technicians for the Dead starting developing a massive sound system designed to provide good sound in large venues. The system was debuted at the Kezar show on May 26, 1973 and was improved and refined until it eventually ended up with 641 speakers, powered by 26,400 watts RMS, at a weight of 25 tons and needing two semi's to transport it. It became known as the "wall of sound" and on March 23, 1974 the completed system was used at the "Sound Test" at the Cow Palace in Daly City. The "wall of sound" had the cleanest sound and widest frequency range of any sound system heard at that time.

Though Grateful Dead Records and its subsidiary, Round Records, put out some notable albums such as the Grateful Dead albums *Wake of the Flood* and *From the Mars Hotel*, and Garcia's solo albums *Reflections* and *Compliments of Garcia*, by the fall of 1974 the band's business ventures began to unravel. Cash-flow problems were common, and the band was suffocating under the weight and cost of transporting around the 25 tons of equipment that made up the "wall of sound." Needing a break from touring and time to regroup, the band announced their decision to retire from performing, and played one last set of shows at Winterland in October of 1974. The shows were filmed for posterity, and Mickey Hart made a guest appearance at the last show, as if to indicate that this might indeed be the final curtain call.

GREG GAAR

Filming at Winterland, October 1974

After a short hiatus the Dead came out of retirement to play at the SNACK benefit, held at Kezar Stadium on March 23, 1975. Appearing under the moniker "Jerry Garcia and Friends," the Dead performed along with Bob Dylan, Neil Young, Joan Baez, and a host of other bands. The funds raised were used to support student athletic and cultural needs that were threatened by budgetary cutbacks. With the assistance of Merl Saunders and Ned Lagin, the Grateful Dead performed a rather avant-garde piece of music that they had been working on called "Blues for Allah." Merl Saunders was a keyboardist who had been performing with Jerry Garcia since early 1971. Ned Lagin was an electronic music wizard, who had performed experimental "electronic cybernetic biomusic" with Phil Lesh at several Dead shows in the fall of 1974, including opening the second sets of their "retirement shows" at Winterland in October 1974.

The Bob Fried Memorial Boogie was held on June 17, 1975 at Winterland in San Francisco to commemorate '60s poster artist Bob Fried. Though the show was promoted as featuring "Jerry Garcia and Friends," Kingfish, and the Keith and Donna Band, expectation was running high that the Grateful Dead would again perform. The audience was not let down as the Dead not only performed, but debuted new songs from their forthcoming album *Blues for Allah*.

GREG GAAR

**Bob Dylan & Neil Young at the 'Snack Benefit,' Kezar Stadium, March 23, 1975**

**Golden Gate Park, September 28, 1975**

To celebrate the release of *Blues for Allah* on September 1, 1975, the first official Grateful Dead show since their retirement was held at the Great American Music Hall in San Francisco on August 13, 1975. In an intimate hall with a seating capacity of 425, a SRO crowd of family members, friends, and music industry people saw the Dead perform in a club-like setting for the first time since the mid-'60s.

In September 1975 the Grateful Dead played a free concert at Lindley Meadows in Golden Gate Park with the Jefferson Starship. The concert drew an estimated 50,000 people and was a throwback to the numerous free concerts performed in Golden Gate Park in the '60s. The Dead and the Starship rose to the occasion and a good time was had by all.

To the delight of their fans the Grateful Dead started touring again in June 1976. With the reintroduction of Mickey Hart into the band, new arrangements of old Grateful Dead songs were worked out, as well as the addition of new material to the repertoire. The band played an extensive tour schedule of sold-out shows and in October 1976 performed with the Who at Oakland Stadium. Reminiscent of shows from the '60s when legendary groups often shared the same bill, the two bands played on consecutive days at the "Day on the Green."

A 'Day on the Green'

The *Grateful Dead Movie* was released on June 1, 1977. The movie starts with an animation sequence that captures the psychedelic experience of the '60s, and then segues into live concert footage. The film portrays what a live Grateful Dead concert is all about. Jerry Garcia spent countless hours supervising the editing of film shot at the Winterland shows in October 1974, and worked with Grateful Dead sound engineer Dan Healy on perfecting the sound track.

On August 12, 1977 at Pier 31 in San Francisco, the Jerry Garcia Band performed a benefit concert for Greenpeace, once again

showing that the '60s ideal of making a better world still survived, even if most of the '60s bands had not. Less than a month later the Dead played to a crowd of over 100,000 people at Raceway Park in Englishtown, New Jersey, confirming that the torchbearers of the '60s were still as popular as ever. The Dead performed songs from their newly released album, *Terrapin Station*. The event was the state of New Jersey's largest outdoor concert ever. Since Grateful Dead Records was no longer a viable business venture, the band signed with Arista Records, which released the album *Terrapin Station*.

The Dead kicked off 1978 by touring California. The tour included a stop at the intimate Arlington Theatre in Santa Barbara on January 13, where the Dead performed a benefit concert for the Pacific Alliance, a group formed to help coordinate the movement away from nuclear power and toward renewable energy sources such as solar, wind, and energy conservation. Leaving California at the end of the tour for one show at the University of Oregon at Eugene, the Dead once again proved "there is nothing like a Grateful Dead concert," by incorporating the beautiful theme to the movie *Close Encounters of the Third Kind* into their show that night.

The Grateful Dead reached another milestone in their long and colorful history in September 1978. The Dead's dream of playing at the pyramids in Egypt was fulfilled when they were granted permission by the Egyptian government to perform three concerts at the Sound and Light Theatre at the foot of the Great Pyramid. The venture cost the band $500,000, and proceeds from the concerts were donated to the Egyptian Department of Antiquities, and to the Faith and Hope Society, an organization that helps the handicapped. A chartered flight from the states brought an entourage of Dead Heads and Dead family to Egypt. Among those who went to Egypt to experience the magic were Ken Kesey, Mountain Girl, Owsley, Nicki Scully, David Freiberg, Bill Graham, and Bill Walton.

The concerts were on September 14-16, 1978, and the Dead performed with Hamza El-Din, an Egyptian oud master,[1] who was a friend of Mickey Hart back in California. Each night Hamza was joined by a group of Nubian musicians who clapped their hands, played a Nubian drum called the tar, and sang. As the Nubian music progressed, various members of the Grateful Dead would join in, and the music segued into a Grateful Dead set. Before the second concert one of the Pranksters, George Walker, climbed the Great Pyramid and placed a Grateful Dead flag at the top for all to see.

The concerts climaxed on the final night of September 16, 1978, with the band performing during a total lunar eclipse of the full moon. After the show ended at approximately 3 a.m., Bill Graham hosted a lavish feast at Sahara City, an hour away by horseback, or fifteen minutes by car. Bob Weir was the first to

---

[1] An oud is a musical instrument in the lute family.

ADRIAN BOOT

**El A-Cid**

arrive by horseback. He was gradually joined by the other members of the Dead entourage who had crossed the desert on horseback and camel. Being a full moon and Kesey's birthday, the evening proceeded in true Prankster style. Kesey, "El A-Cid," attired in Arab dress, was holding court with Jerry Garcia, while Bill Graham and Mickey Hart raced around carrying trays of beer.

After their return from Egypt, the Dead performed five shows at Winterland in San Francisco, and brought some of the magic of the pyramids back to the States. On the last two nights, Hamza El-Din performed, and in a reprise of Egypt, the Dead joined him onstage for a jam that segued into a Grateful Dead set. October 21, 1978 was perhaps the best Grateful Dead show on the West Coast since the '60s, combining the best of what Egypt and the Dead had to offer.

On the afternoon of November 17, 1978, Weir, Garcia, Lesh, and Hart, who were in the Chicago area in the midst of a Grateful Dead tour, played an acoustic set in the Rambler Room at Loyola College in Chicago. Playing for a Hunger Week Benefit with little advance notice, a few hundred lucky people got to see them perform ten acoustic tunes in an intimate setting for a nominal admission charge.

With the closing of Winterland in San Francisco on December 31, 1978, one of the last landmarks of the '60s closed its doors to rock music. The final concert at Winterland, featuring the New Riders, the Blues Brothers, and the Grateful Dead, was an all-night party that marked the closing of the hall. Dead Heads came from

The Closing of Winterland, December 31, 1978

far and wide to attend the occasion, camping in the street to secure a good seat in the hall. Tickets were in great demand and going for $30.00, which at the time was San Francisco's most expensive concert ever. Some of the crowd, covered in costumes and painted faces, was a reminder of the audience in attendance at the Trips Festival at Longshoremen's Hall in 1966.

At the start of the concert, the audience watched Belushi's *Animal House*, followed by the juggling act the Flying Karamozov Brothers and then a set by the New Riders. After an introduction that warned "By the year 2006 the music known today as the blues will exist only in the classical section of your local library," Jake and Elwood Blues (a.k.a. John Belushi and Dan Aykroyd) came out in dark suits, thin black ties, and sunglasses.

MICHAEL ZAGARIS

**The Blues Brothers**

**We Bid You Goodnight**

Their backup band included an all-star lineup of blues musicians, and the Blues Brothers rocked the house with a tight and energetic set. With the beginning of the New Year, and the onslaught of thousands of balloons showering down from the ceiling, the Grateful Dead launched into one of their most memorable performances, playing three sets, and resurrecting "Dark Star," which they had not performed in more than four years. The Dead played until dawn, closing with an a cappella "We Bid You Goodnight." Afterwards the audience was treated to breakfast, courtesy of Bill Graham. In all, it was a fitting ending to a venerable institution like Winterland.

The next Grateful Dead show in the San Francisco Bay area was the "Rock for Life Benefit" initiated by Jane Fonda and Tom Hayden. The proceeds from the concert were used to help their foundation, which is dedicated to ending "environmental cancer." The concert, held on February 17, 1979, marked yet another turning point for the Grateful Dead since it was Keith and Donna

Godchaux's last show with the band. On April 22, 1979 at Spartan Stadium in San Jose, the Grateful Dead introduced keyboardist Brent Mydland. Mydland, an accomplished pianist and organ player, had been a sideman in Bob Weir's band. The band liked his flexibility as a keyboardist and his harmonies, which gave the group a good vocal blend. It was also at this show that the drummers introduced "The Beast," a huge circular rack of drums

'The Beast'

and percussion instruments that was mounted above Kreutzmann and Hart. This enabled the drummers to introduce more variety into their second-set drum solos. Hart, who had long been a collector of exotic drum and percussion instruments, had specifically built "The Beast" for use in making the soundtrack for Francis Ford Coppola's *Apocalypse Now*, a movie about the Vietnam War. Coppola, who wanted to capture the sounds of the Southeast Asian jungle in the film, had contacted Hart to contribute to the soundtrack. Hart enlisted the help of some of his talented friends, like Bill Kreutzmann, Brazilian percussionist Airto, vocalist Flora Purim, and drummer Michael Hinton. They worked for about fifteen days producing a soundtrack that was used throughout parts of the movie.

Hart and Kreutzmann's work on the soundtrack for Coppola's Southeast Asian war saga must have made an impression on them because the Grateful Dead ushered in the new decade of the

GREG GAAR

eighties with a benefit concert for Cambodian refugees. On January 13, 1980 the Dead, the Jefferson Starship, Joan Baez, John Cippolina, and Carlos Santana performed at the Oakland Coliseum to help the refugees of the war in Indochina.

RICK BRACKETT

The Grateful Dead had their official 15th anniversary celebration at the University of Colorado at Boulder on June 7-8, 1980. In attendance were members of the Grateful Dead family, as well as numerous members of the press. Bill Kreutzmann's father was seen backstage sporting a shirt with the logo "Grateful Dad" on it. The band held court at a nearby hotel where they were lodged, partying with any Dead Head savvy enough to find out about it. Bob Weir, obviously in a playful mood, was playing hide and seek with a Dead Head of the female persuasion, who was feeling no pain and was in no shape to keep up with him. Jerry Garcia was in the hospitality room, freely rapping with anyone who wandered in, and John Barlow, Grateful Dead lyricist, was being queried about the mysteries of writing lyrics for a 1960s psychedelic rock band. In the bar various band members and roadies imbibed and had a good time with whomever happened by. It was a generous way for a legendary rock band to celebrate their 15th anniversary with their fans.

As if fate were looking over their shoulders, at the very next concert in Portland, Oregon on June 12, 1980, the Dead kicked off the second set with "Scarlet Begonias" which segued into "Fire on the Mountain" as Mt. Saint Helens erupted and spewed smoke and volcanic ash for miles around. Leaving the concert in a snowstorm of volcanic ash, Dead Heads had to wonder if the band's song selection that night had played any role in the sudden eruption.

John Barlow

One short week later on June 19-21, 1980 the band played in the friendly confines of West High Auditorium in Anchorage, Alaska, to a small audience of Dead Heads, most of whom had flown there from the lower forty-eight to see their favorite rock band. During the summer solstice in that northern latitude, the sun never fully set, and it made a beautiful backdrop for a three-day '60s-style celebration. Spotting Garcia at the baggage terminal at Anchorage Airport upon arrival, an inquisitive Dead Head asked him if the band was going to mark the occasion of the Summer Solstice in Alaska by playing "Dark Star." Garcia politely responded, "I wouldn't count on it, man." Nonetheless, those in attendance had a memorable time.

Not to be outdone by nature, the Grateful Dead played a run of fifteen shows at the Warfield Theatre in San Francisco which were followed by two shows at the Saenger Arts Center in New Orleans, and eight shows at Radio City Music Hall in New York City. The run of twenty-five shows began on September 25, 1980 at the Warfield and ended Halloween night at Radio City Music Hall. At each of the shows the Dead brought out the acoustic guitars and performed acoustic sets for the first time since 1970. In addition, Franken and Davis of *Saturday Night Live* fame were brought on board to spice things up. Preparing numerous gags around Grateful Dead folklore and mythology, the two comedians perfected skits at the Warfield shows to be used for filming in New York for a closed circuit simulcast on Halloween night. One skit revolved around a takeoff of Jerry's kids, with various Dead Heads appearing as Garcia's poster kids.

Bill Graham, in an act of ultimate class, brought champagne to the last show of the Warfield run, and when the band was backstage during the last set, he had his people discreetly serve champagne to each of the members of the audience. When the Dead came out on stage they noticed a table with a bucket of champagne and glasses on it. With the house lights dimmed, the band was unaware of what was going on and figured they were supposed to toast the crowd, but upon raising their glasses, saw to their amazement the audience toast them *en masse* instead. To help celebrate their 15th anniversary, the Dead and Bill Graham donated the proceeds from the final concert to various worthy charities, including the Haight-Ashbury Free Clinic, the Abalone Alliance, and the Planet Drum Foundation.

The filming of the Radio City shows went so well that the Dead produced two different 90-minute versions featuring a selection of acoustic and electric songs, as well as some Franken and Davis comedy routines involving members of the band. One version was sold as a special for Showtime TV while the other was marketed as a commercial video.

The Grateful Dead's New Year's run of shows at the Oakland

Auditorium included a benefit for the Seva Foundation, a non-profit organization which was formed with the assistance of Wavy Gravy to help relieve suffering around the world. Seva, a Sanskrit word that means service to mankind, supports a variety of causes aimed at helping those in need.

In the spring of 1981 the Grateful Dead traveled to Europe and ended a short tour by playing with the Who at the Grugahalle, in Essen, West Germany. Legendary rock guitarist Pete Townsend came onstage during the Dead's set. Garcia and Townsend, two of the great lead guitarists from the '60s, played dueling guitars as Townsend jammed with the Dead on five songs.

Performing at the University of Oregon on August 16, 1981, the Dead were joined on stage by Ken Kesey, Zane Kesey, and Ken Babbs, who brought out the Thunder Machine during the drum solo, and added the Prankster touch to the show. Designed by sculptor Ron Boise, the Thunder Machine was a leftover from the Acid Tests of the '60s.

JAY BLAKESBERG

**Kesey & the Thunder Machine**

RON DELANY

Returning to Europe for a more extended tour in the fall, the Dead celebrated Bob Weir's birthday on October 16, 1981 at the Melk Weg in Amsterdam, by playing an acoustic set and then coming back with a wild electric set that was a throwback to the '60s. Performing "Hully Gully," "Gloria," and the first "Lovelight" since Pigpen's death, the band left no doubt that spur-of-the-moment, impromptu jamming was still part of their musical repertoire.

Played in front of a tie-dye backdrop, the Grateful Dead concerts at the Greek Theatre in September 1981 were a clear reminder of the colorful '60s. The backdrop was fashioned by tie-dye artist Courtenay Pollack, who had decorated the Dead's speakers and amplifier covers in the '60s. Similar tie-dye backdrops were used at the Dead's Greek Theatre shows in following years.

**Tie-Dye Speaker Covers**

The Grateful Dead performed at the San Mateo County Fairgrounds with longtime friend Joan Baez on December 12, 1981 in a concert called "The Dance for Disarmament." Baez, an advocate of nonviolence, has worked tirelessly for the causes of peace, civil rights, and human rights. In the mid-'60s Baez and Ira Sandperl formed the Institute for the Study of Nonviolence, which was dedicated to studying and teaching the principles of nonviolence. Baez also gave her time to the Bread and Roses Foundation, an organization that her sister Mimi Farina founded which brings entertainment into prisons, hospitals, retirement homes, and other institutions. At the Dance for Disarmament concert the Dead backed Baez for her acoustic set, then came back for an electric set. A couple of weeks later Baez again joined the Dead, and performed with them at the Oakland Auditorium on December 30-31, 1981.

At a show in Hartford, Connecticut on April 18, 1982 the Grateful Dead proved once again that no two of their shows are ever alike. After the end of the drum solo Phil Lesh grabbed a microphone and started raving about the San Francisco Earthquake of 1906 in a style reminiscent of a Prankster's rap. The following night in Baltimore at the end of the drum solo Lesh started reciting the "Raven" by Edgar Allan Poe.

Joan Baez

As the only surviving San Francisco '60s band, the Dead's commitment to worthy causes stayed forever strong. On May 28, 1982 the Grateful Dead performed at the Vietnam Vets Benefit with Airto, Flora Purim, John Cippolina, and Boz Scaggs. Another worthy cause came to their attention in August 1982. The Oregon Country Faire was the prototype for the Renaissance Faire in California. Every summer, thousands of people came to land near Veneta, Oregon, to camp in the woods, display crafts, and discuss environmental issues. To avoid the eventual hassle of losing the lease to the land where the fair is held, the board that ran the fair decided to try to purchase the land when it was put up for sale. The Dead agreed to perform a concert to help with its purchase. With Kesey and the Springfield Creamery lending a helping hand, the Second Decadenal Field Trip was held with the Grateful Dead performing on August 28, 1982. The proceeds from the concert were used to purchase the land for the Oregon Country Faire.

In November 1982 the Dead traveled to Montego Bay, Jamaica, to perform at the World Music Festival. On a chartered flight from San Francisco, an entourage of Dead family members and Dead Heads made the trip. Wavy Gravy was along for the ride, and, in typical Prankster fashion, the Dead Heads commandeered the flight and headed off into the wild blue yonder. The aircraft became a real zoo as Dead Heads, Clash Heads, and Rasta Heads boomed their ghetto blasters simultaneously to the chagrin of the few other passengers on the plane. The Grateful Dead performed on the same bill with reggae artists Jimmy Cliff, Peter Tosh, and a host of other bands. The Dead used a boat as their backstage area, and played into the wee hours of the morning at the Bob Marley Memorial.

To close out the year in style the Dead performed an entire set with blues great Etta James at the New Year's show at the Oakland Auditorium. Accompanied by the Tower of Power horn

**Etta James, Tower of Power & the Grateful Dead**

section, the ensemble performed five rocking blues numbers including "Lovelight," "Hard to Handle," and "Midnight Hour," songs that the Dead had performed frequently during Pigpen's tenure with the band.

During the spring tour of the East coast in 1983 the Dead performed with Stephen Stills, an original member of the '60s group Buffalo Springfield, who went on to help form Crosby, Stills, and Nash. At two concerts at the Brendan Byrne Arena in New Jersey, Stills came out each night after the drum solo to jam with the band he refers to as "the world's greatest garage band."

**Stephen Stills**

The Dead returned to Oregon in August 1983 in the middle of a thirteen-show tour and played three sold-out shows at the Hult Center, a small hall in Eugene. The Hult Center was the smallest venue on the tour and many traveling Dead Heads got shut out of the shows. Dead Heads inundated the Hilton Hotel adjacent to the concert site, much to the management's dismay; but in true '60s spirit the management opened up the hotel rather than resist the onslaught. Dead Heads displayed their wares in the lobby, and generally took over the place, while members of the band who also happened to be staying at the hotel mingled with the fans in the lobby.

On October 30-31, 1983, the Dead played in their hometown of San Rafael for the first time since 1970, performing at the intimate Marin County Veterans Auditorium. The crowd was in a festive mood, and on Halloween night many were adorned in costume and makeup, with more than one Jerry Garcia and conehead running around the auditorium. Playing to an audience of only 2,000, the Dead dazzled the crowd with an incredible show that included "St. Stephen" and ended with the Beatles' song "Revolution."

Returning to the Marin County Veterans Auditorium in March, the Dead played their first concerts of 1984. These shows were the first benefit shows for the Rex Foundation, a nonprofit charitable organization established in 1984 to make contributions to creative endeavors in the arts, sciences, education, and in the area of social exchange and healing. Named in honor of Rex Jackson, a road crew member who died in a car accident in 1976, the Rex Foundation is not legally affiliated with the band, but members of the Dead family assist in its operation. The Foundation's board of directors includes Jerry Garcia, Bob Weir, Carolyn Garcia, John Barlow, Bill Graham, and Bill Walton.

Keeping Prankster tradition alive, Ken Kesey and Ken Babbs showed up for one of the Dead's concerts in Eugene in May 1984. With champagne available in the lobby, the crowd loved every minute of the madness that the Thunder Machine's eclectic sounds added to the drum solo that evening.

At the Berkeley Community Theatre in October 1984, the Grateful Dead instituted the "Tapers Section," an area specifically set aside for the taping of the band by members of the audience. While most record companies and bands frown upon the tape recording of live performances because of the assumption that it hurts record sales, the Grateful Dead realized that the taping of their live concerts was an integral part of the Dead Head subculture and at each concert the Dead set aside a section of seats, or

Berkeley Community Theatre, October 1984

RON DELANY

an area of the arena, for tapers. In so doing, the band sanctioned the taping of concerts, and also eliminated the incidental disruption of the concert for the non-taping audience by overzealous tapers. The taping of concerts by Dead Heads had been going on since the '60s, and certainly helped contribute to the legions of dedicated fans. It should be noted that Garcia, in his early days as a bluegrass picker, spent time collecting and swapping tapes.

The second set of Rex Foundation shows was in March 1985 at the Berkeley Community Theatre. On March 9, Merl Saunders played with the Dead, and in an improvisational jam out of the drums, Garcia played the *Twilight Zone* theme, a theme he was very familiar with since he contributed to the opening soundtrack of the reborn TV series.

The high point of 1985 was the unofficial 20th Anniversary Show held at the Greek Theatre on June 14, 1985. From the first notes of the introduction played on the PA by soundman Dan Healy, the Beatles' "It was twenty years ago today, Sgt. Pepper taught the band to play," it was obvious the band was taking the anniversary seriously. The crowd was in an upbeat and raucous mood, and when the Dead broke into "Dancin' in the Streets," a song straight out of the '60s, the audience went wild. The band couldn't have picked a more perfect song to open the show and retrace their roots.

RON DELANY

The Greek Theatre, Berkeley, June 1985

During their summer tour of 1985, the Dead made a stop at Morrison, Colorado to play at the Red Rocks Amphitheater in the foothills of the Rocky Mountains. Performing in one of the most beautiful venues in the country, the band played the "Hey Jude" finale during the show on September 7. One of the Beatles' classic songs, it superbly captures the idealism and spirit of the '60s and was a perfect song for the Dead to add to their repertoire. The song was a real flashback for those aging hippies in the crowd who were still on the bus.

The Grateful Dead ended their anniversary year with a national TV broadcast of their show from the Oakland Coliseum on December 31, 1985. The Neville Brothers opened the show. Known as musician's musicians, the Nevilles' sound is culled from a variety of styles — jazz, Caribbean, African, Cajun, and rock.

New Year's Eve, December 31, 1985

RON DELANY

Charles Neville calls their music New Orleans rhythm and blues. It has an infectious beat, inspiring Neville Brothers fans to dance with reckless abandon at their concerts, an activity not unfamiliar to fans of the Grateful Dead. Following the Neville Brothers set, Baba Olatunji performed his percussive magic for the crowd. Starting with the countdown to midnight, the viewing audience around the country, including Hawaii, was treated to a Grateful Dead New Year's Eve Party. Handling the microphone as commentators were none other than the Merry Prankster himself, Ken Kesey, and the big-red Dead Head, Bill Walton. With commentary reminiscent of a Neal Cassady speed-rap, Kesey led the audience into the New Year wondering if it was 1966 or 1986.

Bill Graham as Father Time

While 1985 was a milestone year for the Grateful Dead, the year to follow would prove even more eventful. The first run of shows at the Kaiser Convention Center in Oakland in February saw the Neville Brothers on the bill again with the Dead for two of the shows to help celebrate Mardi Gras. The Neville Brothers complement the Dead perfectly so it was not surprising to see them jamming with the Dead at these two shows.

**The Neville Brothers**

News of the Grateful Dead's summer tour with Bob Dylan and his backup group, Tom Petty and the Heartbreakers, generated great excitement that spring. The big question was whether the tour would produce the first Dead-Dylan musical collaboration. Garcia was a longtime fan of Dylan's music, and the Dead had been performing his tunes as early as 1965. With the advent of summer, the excitement mounted. At the first show of the summer tour in Minneapolis, though on the same bill, Dylan and the Dead did not jam together. However, on July 2, 1986 at the University of Akron during the Dead's first set Dylan came out on stage with his guitar and sat in with the Dead on "Little Red Rooster," "Don't Think Twice, It's Alright," and "It's All Over Now, Baby Blue." On July 7, 1986 Dylan and the Dead performed together on "It's All Over Now, Baby Blue" and "Desolation Row" at RFK Stadium in Washington, D.C. By the end of the tour it appeared that a more involved collaboration was close at hand.

Then on July 10, 1986, Jerry Garcia, who was suffering from the onset of diabetes and dehydration, fell into a diabetic coma. Found unconscious at his home in San Rafael, he was rushed to Marin General Hospital where he was attended to by waiting physicians. The doctors' initial prognosis was guarded, and a 24-hour vigil began with some of his closest friends in attendance. When word of Garcia's condition reached the public, a massive outpouring of love and positive energy was sent his way. The coma lasted five days, and upon his awakening, his legions of fans breathed a collective sigh of relief. Steve Parish, his longtime confidant, brought Garcia his guitar and the doctors marveled at his miraculous recovery.

Upon his release from the hospital, Garcia started spending afternoons with his friend, keyboardist Merl Saunders, and worked on regaining his chops. In the midst of his recuperation, Garcia headed up to Eugene to hang out with his Prankster pal Ken Babbs for a little rest and relaxation.

That old Prankster magic must have worked, because on December 15, 1986, the music played the band again. As the first notes of "Touch of Grey" rang out, the sold-out crowd at the Oakland Coliseum exploded in rapturous approval; when Garcia sang "I will survive" there was not a dry eye in the house. On

RON DELANY

Oakland Coliseum, December 1986

December 16, members of the Neville Brothers jammed with the Dead to celebrate Garcia's triumphant return as the "Grandfather" of rock and roll.

Closing out the year with a run of four shows at the Kaiser Convention Center, the Neville Brothers shared the bill with the Grateful Dead on all four nights. On New Year's Eve David Crosby also performed. A joyous crowd was extremely happy to bring in another year with their spiritual adviser, Captain Trips.

**Captain Trips**

In 1987 the Grateful Dead began touring the country again and dispelled any doubt that Garcia was healthy and ready to rock and roll. Rumors of the long-awaited Dead-Dylan collaboration started to spread with word of Dylan's presence at the Dead's studio in San Rafael. With the Dead performing Dylan's "All Along the Watchtower" for the first time on June 20, 1987 at the Greek Theatre in Berkeley, the historic moment was close at hand. Dylan and the Dead began a six-city tour of sold-out stadiums on

Dylan & the Dead

RON DELANY

the East and West coasts on July 4, 1987. The Dead performed their own set at each show and then performed with Dylan for a lengthy set of his classic material. Playing in a style that was distinctively Dead, but reminiscent of the Band, Garcia's guitar work gave the ballads an easy and relaxed feel and gave the rockers, like "All Along the Watchtower," a driving and uplifting force.

The Grateful Dead released the album *In the Dark* on July 6, 1987. Its release coincided with the 20th anniversary of the Summer of Love, and confirmed that the band from the '60s was still gathering strength as legions of new Dead Heads got "on the bus" and made *In the Dark* a platinum album. Included on the album was "Throwing Stones," a song penned by John Barlow, which addressed the issue of planetary survival in the wake of the proliferation of nuclear weapons.

After the conclusion of the Dead-Dylan tour, the Grateful Dead headed for the beautiful environs of the Rocky Mountains in Colorado. Performing at Red Rocks Amphitheater and then at Town Park in Telluride, the band was in a gracious mood, no doubt inspired by the majestic surroundings. Members of the Dead mingled with the crowd between the Telluride shows in a relaxed atmosphere reminiscent of the days when they could casually walk down Haight Street and engage people in friendly conversation.

BRIAN GOLD

Telluride, Colorado

**Aids Benefit, December 17, 1987**

Carlos Santana played with the Grateful Dead the weekend of August 22-23, 1987 at Angel's Camp, California. Santana opened the show, and then came out during the Dead's set to jam on a number of songs, including "Good Morning Little Schoolgirl," an old blues tune that appeared on the Dead's first album, but which the band had not performed since 1970.

*So Far*, a Grateful Dead film directed by Len Dell'Amico and Jerry Garcia, was released in October 1987. The film blends band footage, animation and visual images to deliver a strong anti-war message and address modern society's degradation of the environment. Though the Dead have been known to be apolitical, the film has a strong political and social statement to offer.

Joan Baez, always active in helping philanthropic causes, organized a concert to benefit AIDS research that was held at the Warfield Theatre on December 17, 1987. Jerry Garcia, Bob Weir, and John Kahn performed as an acoustic trio for the first time doing a number of tunes, and then were joined onstage by Joan Baez, who provided backup vocals to three songs. At the close of the show Garcia and Weir joined in with Baez to sing a beautiful version of the Beatles' "Let It Be."

At the New Year's show at the Oakland Coliseum on December 31, 1987, Justin Kreutzmann, son of Bill Kreutzmann, and Gabe Harris, son of Joan Baez, handled some of the live commentary for the TV broadcast of the show which was carried across the country. The Neville Brothers were again in attendance to

open the festivities and jammed with the Dead during the third set of the evening. Also in attendance were Ken Kesey and Mountain Girl, who helped bring in the New Year in fine Prankster tradition.

The Grateful Dead began 1988 with two sets of shows at the

GENE ANTHONY

Kaiser Convention Center. After the last Kaiser show the Dead toured extensively, maintaining their position as one of the top-grossing touring bands in the country.

To commemorate the end of a coast-to-coast United States-Soviet peace walk, a free concert was held in Golden Gate Park in San Francisco on July 16, 1988. About 20,000 people saw a variety of Soviet and San Francisco musicians play, including Jerry

Paul Kantner, Grace Slick & Mickey Hart

Garcia, Mickey Hart, Paul Kantner, Grace Slick, and John Cippolina. Later that day at the Greek Theatre in Berkeley, Soviet pop artist Alexander Gradsky performed a Russian folk song between Grateful Dead sets. Although he sang in his native tongue, his music apparently transcended language barriers, as the song was well received by the crowd.

One of the highlights of the year came when the Dead played

**Alexander Gradsky**

nine sold-out shows at Madison Square Garden in New York City. The last show was a benefit concert for the Rain Forest Action Network, Greenpeace, and Cultural Survival. The Grateful Dead held a press conference at the United Nations on September 14, 1988 to explain the purpose of the benefit concert, which was meant to remind people that the ongoing destruction of the rain forests could threaten global survival. Performing at the benefit with the Grateful Dead were Bruce Hornsby and the Range, Mick Taylor, Suzanne Vega, Daryl Hall and John Oates, Jack Casady, Baba Olatunji, and Michael Hinton. The benefit on September 24, 1988 raised $600,000 to help save the world's vanishing rain forests. Dr. Noel Brown, the head of the United Nations Environmental Program, said the Dead's involvement had brought more press attention to the issue than he had seen in the previous ten years.

As the Grateful Dead entered the last year of the decade, it seemed that their commitment to helping make a better world had never been stronger. At the first show of the year at the Kaiser Convention Center in Oakland on February 5, 1989, Garcia debuted a new song written by Robert Hunter, "Standing on the Moon," which poignantly depicts the violence on our planet, but at the same time offers a sense of hope and optimism. At the same show Brent Mydland debuted another new song, "We Can Run," penned by John Barlow, which clearly points out that with global survival at stake, mankind must take responsibility for the world's problems.

In May 1989 the Dead performed two benefit shows for the Rex Foundation at the Frost Amphitheatre in Palo Alto. The Frost is a beautiful grass-covered amphitheater surrounded by trees on the Stanford University campus. A wonderful venue to see a show, it exudes a feeling of nostalgia and history since Palo Alto is where the Grateful Dead got their start. The concerts were broadcast on the college radio station and in the eucalyptus grove next to the amphitheater the sounds of the concert could be heard not only directly from the stage, but also on the multitude of radios tuned into the broadcast. This created a strange psychoacoustic effect reminiscent of the multi-speakered sound system that the Pranksters devised in the woods surrounding La Honda.

The In Concert Against Aids benefit was held at Oakland Stadium on May 27, 1989. There were several bands on the bill, including the Grateful Dead, John Fogerty, the founding member

of Creedence Clearwater Revival, Tracy Chapman, and Joe Satriani. In an historical meeting of '60s legends, Fogerty had a backup band that included Jerry Garcia and Bob Weir. The concert helped to bring the community together in the fight against AIDS.

RON DELANY

TIM MOSENFELDER

JG & John Fogerty

John Cippolina, one of the legendary musicians from the '60s San Francisco psychedelic rock scene, died on May 29, 1989. The lead guitarist of Quicksilver Messenger Service, Cippolina's distinctive guitar lines helped define the San Francisco sound. After leaving Quicksilver in October 1970, Cippolina formed several bands, and in 1982 joined the Dinosaurs, an all-star group that was made up of members from several of the great '60s San Francisco psychedelic rock bands: Barry Melton from Country Joe and the Fish on guitar, Peter Albin from Big Brother and the Holding Company on bass, Spencer Dryden from the Jefferson Airplane on drums, and Robert Hunter, the Grateful Dead lyricist, on guitar.

MICHAEL ZAGARIS

**John Cippolina**

The 20th anniversary of Woodstock was celebrated in August 1989 with a plethora of events and media attention. The Jefferson Airplane re-formed for the first time since the early '70s and toured on both the East and West coasts during the summer of 1989. The band performed their classic '60s hits as well as some new songs. Always known as a very politically conscious band, their new songs addressed global political problems, as well as various environmental issues. Grace Slick performed a new song she wrote called "Panda," which tells the story of the panda's danger of extinction, while Marty Balin sang "Solidarity," a song he wrote in collaboration with playwright and political visionary Bertholt Brecht. The song speaks about the notion of forging a global consciousness to attack the world's problems. The Airplane also performed a Paul Kantner song called "America," which addresses the problem of the hungry and homeless people in the streets of our nation, the wealthiest country on earth.

Not content to let their songs alone do the work for them, the Airplane performed a free concert on September 30, 1989 at the Polo Field in Golden Gate Park to benefit the San Francisco Food Bank. Performing to a crowd of 60,000 on a gorgeous Saturday afternoon, the event was a flashback to the halcyon days of the '60s when free concerts were a common phenomenon. Bob Weir and Rob Wasserman opened the show with an acoustic set.

The free concert netted the San Francisco Food Bank the most massive single-day haul in its history as concert-goers donated 45,000 pounds of canned food to provide more than 40,000 meals to help the needy at shelters, hospices, and soup kitchens around the city. One week later the Airplane performed at a rally at the United States Capitol in Washington, D.C. to protest the plight of the homeless in our country. A crowd of about 40,000 took to the streets to protest repeated cuts in the federal housing budget and to demand affordable housing for low-income Americans. Along with an array of celebrities, the Airplane gave their support to a cause they believe in.

Another flashback to the '60s occurred on the nights of October 8-9, 1989 when the Grateful Dead performed as the Warlocks at the Hampton Coliseum in Hampton, Virginia, because of opposition by the local authorities to the Grateful Dead performing there. The Dead had not performed using that name since 1965 when they were the house band for the Acid Tests. To mark the occasion the Dead performed "Dark Star" at the second show in Hampton, which was the first time they had played it since July 13, 1984 at the Greek Theatre in Berkeley. The October 9, 1989 concert was considered by many Dead Heads to be the best of the decade.

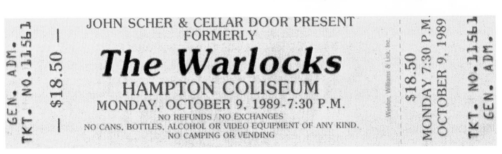

With the decade drawing to a close the Grateful Dead addressed the issues of war, ecology, and planetary survival in their album *Built to Last* which was released on October 31, 1989. The social and political consciousness of the '60s, which had been dormant in American politics for more than a decade, began to show signs of life and the Dead kept playing on.

Bruce Hornsby & the Dead at the Los Angeles Forum, December 10, 1989

## CAROLYN "MOUNTAIN GIRL" GARCIA

MG, as she is known by her friends, was one of the Merry Pranksters and a close associate of Ken Kesey. She met Jerry Garcia at the Acid Tests in 1965. In early 1967 MG and Jerry started living together and eventually got married and had two daughters. MG has fond memories of her days as a Prankster amid Acid Tests, the Grateful Dead, and high times.

**ST:** Why don't you tell me how you got involved with Ken Kesey?

**MG:** I moved to Palo Alto in 1963 and met Neal Cassady and the Pranksters in 1964. We had this idea to give away LSD free to people at events that we were going to set up. It grew out of a party idea, a Saturday night party. Every Saturday night you have a colossal party and you invite anybody and everybody you can think of to invite and turn them all on and have a good time and show weird movies, light shows, or anything we could think of at the time to do.

**ST:** What year was this?

**MG:** 1965. The Grateful Dead got pulled in because they were also in Palo Alto at the beginning. Jerry played in bluegrass bands, and jug bands.

**ST:** Where were you living at the time?

**MG:** I was living at Kesey's house in La Honda with the Pranksters, with the bus up in the mountains outside of Palo Alto. The Grateful Dead had just come together as a rock and roll band called the Warlocks.

**ST:** Who was in the band?

**MG:** Jerry, Weir, Lesh, Pigpen, and Kreutzmann. Some of them had previously worked together in the jug band. Page Browning of the Pranksters knew Jerry and Phil and knew that they were crazy enough to do something just for kicks. He called them up and told them we were having this great scene down in San Jose, why don't you guys come along and bring your instruments and play. So they went. It was such an amazing trip. The band played, everybody got high, weird, and strange. Some people took their clothes off and it spilled out into the street.

**ST:** Was this the first Acid Test?

**MG:** The early Acid Tests were at Kesey's place and there was also one at Babbs' place. We did them for three or four weeks before we took it to San Jose. LSD was legal then and people were taking big doses. This was a year after the bus came back from New York from the trip with the Pranksters that's chronicled in the Prankster movie *The Merry Pranksters Search for the Cool Place*, the home movies, and in the book *The Electric Kool-Aid Acid Test*.

San Jose was the first public Acid Test in 1965. It was a complete blowout — manic bash. Nobody forgot it — it was cataclysmic! The Pranksters got the idea we could do it, regularly, so we went ahead and did more after that.

**ST:** Wasn't there an Acid Test at Muir Beach?

**MG:** The Muir Beach Acid Test was gorgeous because it was in a big lodge right by the ocean, in two big rooms. The Grateful Dead played. This friend of mine, Owsley, got very high; for an hour or more he was pushing a chair around on a wooden floor. It made a noise that was so bad and so painful and so horrifying that I must have sent six people over to get him to stop. He'd stop for a minute and then get back on the chair and start screeching around the floor some more — the kind of trip people get into which is utterly unpleasant to be anywhere near. It was hard to deal with. The Muir Beach Acid Test was the one where a lot of people reached the cosmos for the first time because it was out in the country, right at the beach, beautiful flowers, shrubs, and green lawn going down to a spectacular moonlit beach. It was gorgeous, really beautiful. It was wonderful and mystical — unforgettable. All sorts of things happened to people there like visits from aliens, getting attacked by grizzlies and Big Foot. Muir Beach was the Acid Test that changed people the deepest, I think. That was the one where Pigpen got dosed. Usually he would get drunk and play because he didn't like acid. It made his fingers all rubbery and he couldn't feel the keys on the keyboard.

**ST:** What was Pigpen like?

**MG:** Pigpen was a stoned, crazy guy from the beginning. He'd get drunk and talk blues. You couldn't help but love Pigpen. He was loveable and everybody liked him. He sang like an old blues singer. It wasn't so much what he sang, it was how he was singing it. He had a lot of soul.

It was sure sad to lose him. We all thought he was getting better. Pigpen wouldn't tell anyone how sick he was. The only person that knew that something was seriously wrong was the photographer, Bob Seidemann. He was the band's photographer. Pigpen invited him over and they went out for a drive and halfway to wherever they were going Pig says, "Wait, stop, get out and take my picture" and he did and it was the last picture ever taken of Pigpen. He died a couple of days later.

**ST:** Wasn't Pigpen the front man for the Grateful Dead in the early days?

**MG:** Pigpen did most of the singing, Jerry sang about a quarter of the tunes, and Weir sang a quarter of the tunes. Pigpen sang half because they liked to do those long stretched-out things he did. In the course of five or six hours, which is how long

Acid Test without them and it didn't work. It wasn't the same without the band.

ST: What were the lights like at the Acid Tests?
MG: We had a powerful strobe light, which I ran along with the projector. I was the master projector runner. We showed films of the bus trip, people getting high, pictures of weird sculptures made of day-glo, films people shot when they were high, sculptures twisting and twinkling in the breeze, feathers and beads and broken glass, pictures of the bus, just crazy stuff. We always had the bus there.

ST:  What was Kesey's bus like?

MG:  The bus was a 1939 International Harvester. It had a turret on the back, an old dryer drum from a laundromat, which was welded on and cut away so that there was a ladder on the inside of the bus that went up to the top and there was a platform with a railing around it on the roof. There was a P.A. system with speakers mounted up there with microphone wires and stereo earphones. You could broadcast music and talk to each other on the headsets going down the highway at 60 mph. There was a car windshield stuck across the front so that you could lie up there without

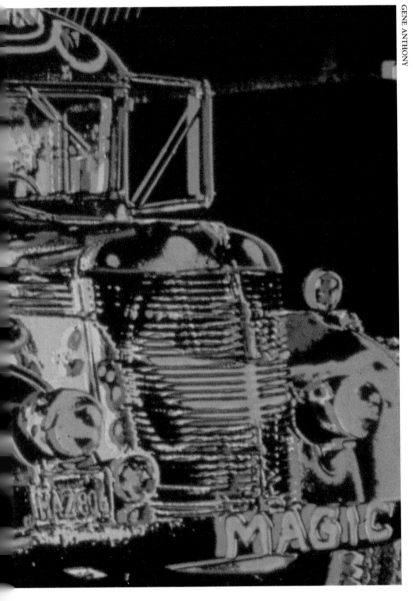

getting your hair blown out. There were two mattresses up there. It was a wonderful place to lie down and smoke joints.

The bus was painted in the most bizarre patterns, random squiggles in day-glo colors. It was a painting that changed and evolved daily. George and I would always paint a while on the bus every morning or whenever we could. When people saw it on the road, there were different reactions:

- Some stood absolutely still and acted like they hadn't seen it — in other words, put in a trance by it as it goes by so they don't even indicate that they saw it.
- Other people couldn't take their eyes off of it. They would watch it but they were frozen in movement, but they were watching it.
- Another kind, they flip out, go crazy, dancing and throwing things in the air. They just loved it.
- There were also those people who thought the bus was too far out. One time we were cruising around the Sierras in the middle of the night, and we came to an intersection. There was this cop on the other side of the road and when we pulled up, he was looking so hard at us that he ran right into the stop sign. It was a classic!

ST: Did people come to the Acid Tests all painted up?

MG: Absolutely. Once they got the idea of what was going on. The first time you'd see them they would be nice and conservative, a sport coat, blue shirt. The next time we did it the dress had gone completely over, into insanity. It was wonderful. Women would jewel their faces by pasting jewels around. There was a lot of face and body painting too. We had a big case of day-glo poster paint. Lots of black lights! We had a corner set up with the day-glo paints. We had it in cups with paint brushes but most people stuck their fingers in it because when you got the stuff on yourself, you looked completely unreal. Your skin disappeared into the glow.

One time we scored this female bust of white plastic and painted it with day-glo and dressed it up. We gave it this amazing contorted day-glo tattoo that continuously evolved. Great stuff!

At dawn Sunday we'd have to clean the place up. It was so much of a scene to see what people had done. Patterns of fingerprints on the wall where somebody had stood for an hour with his finger, marking dots on the wall. It was

GENE ANTHONY

great! Day-glo barefoot prints wandering off. It was really, really good. Everybody had a ball. We had very few freak-outs. We had real good Sandoz acid which was absolutely pure. It didn't mess you up in any way. It was extremely visual and very joyous and happy.

**ST:** What came after the Fillmore Acid Test?

**MG:** I think the Trips Festival. The Trips Festival in downtown San Francisco at Longshoremen's Hall, which is this amazing sort of eagle-winged, concrete, modern structure. A very avant-garde kind of place compared to other halls. Bill Graham had control of the door at this event. He was a maniac. He sold tickets and insisted people have tickets. He was like the antagonist for the free trip, but at the same time he was on our side, working for us.

The Trips Festival was a big production spectacle that

GENE ANTHONY

lasted several days and was run by Stewart Brand and David Singer, who brought in all different kinds of people. His trip was to collect the best from everyone and put it into some kind of package. We trusted him.

Stewart was able to bring in people that none of us knew anything about, like the quiet intellectual who invents a light organ in his closet. Stewart went to him and got him to come down. An incredible light organ that filled up a quarter of this colossal room. It was beautiful. There were many screens and all different kinds of movies being shown. Thirty-five hundred people came to it.

The Grateful Dead played. Neal Cassady was the main announcer, the mad commentator who gave the blow by blow. His entire life force was behind him. He was beautiful at the Trips Festival and the Acid Tests. We'd give him the microphone and a spotlight and some brilliant piece of clothing to shred. He'd do weird scat singing if the music wasn't happening. He'd talk or give commentaries on the girls. Just constant entertainment. He moved fast and loved dancing in the strobe light babbling all this comic rap stuff.

One thing that people used to do at the Acid Tests was to throw things in the air, like a roll of toilet paper. You could throw it across the room and somebody else would see it coming. It would unravel, this beautiful long streamer behind it, and someone would catch it and throw it to someone else while its going. It's really beautiful. You get six or eight of these going and it brings the room together in this soft beautiful way. You're really inside that room, looking out and seeing what's going on in that room. It's like a huge colossal game. The Acid Tests were room games. There was lots of crawling on your hands and knees on the floor, laughing.

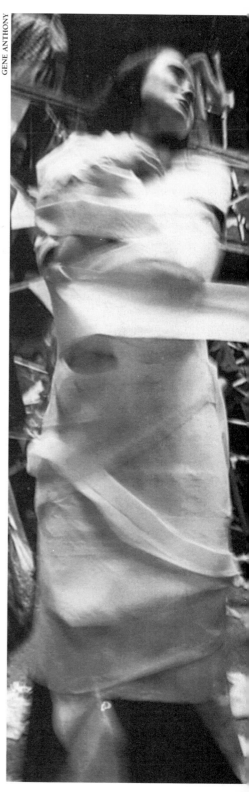

**ST:** Were there any other Acid Tests that stand out?

**MG:** At San Francisco State in October 1966, Kesey did a mystery broadcast and the Grateful Dead played. We had just

Wavy Gravy at the S.F. Acid Test,
October 2, 1966

come back from Mexico. That's when I established a relationship with Jerry. I moved in with him at 710 Ashbury Street in San Francisco a few months later. It was a neat place. An old Victorian house with crumbling stairs. Lilies growing out in front. We tried to fix the place up. Rock, one of their managers, had the apartment downstairs. They had the whole house. Laird, who was their roadie and did their equipment for a long time, lived there. And Matthews, a 16-year-old electronics whiz runaway from the Peninsula, sleeping in a green chair, downstairs, in Weir's room.

Pigpen had a little room around the back of the kitchen and Jerry had a room upstairs with an American flag on one wall that was the size of the whole wall. At that time Jerry was clean shaven. Phil and Kreutzmann had their own place

in Diamond Heights. It was a big family scene. I cooked and we all ate together. Tangerine, who was Rock's old lady, lived there too. Veronica, Pig's girl, was in and out. There were great scenes on the front porch every morning. Everybody from the street would come up and rap with us.

ST: Where was the band playing at that time?

MG: Well, this was late 1966 and early 1967, and mostly the band was playing around San Francisco. They played at the Matrix, Fillmore, the Avalon, the Family Dog, anywhere they could. Each band member made $50 a week.

ST: Was the band popular at this point in time?

MG: Yes and no. Often the hall would be nearly empty during the second set. They did get airplay from a demo disc that was out, "Stealin'," and they were doing free gigs.

ST: How did the free gigs come about?

MG: They'd rent flatbed trucks and line them up, end to end, with a stack of speaker columns at each end and the band in the middle. It made a good stage. The Diggers became adept at this truck trip at short notice. Like Saturday morning, Jerry would get up and say, "Oh, it's a beautiful day. Hey, let's play," and they would pull it together by two in the afternoon because it was like a guerrilla event and there was no media advertising. They'd play at Golden Gate Park, the Polo Fields, the Panhandle, and Lindley Meadows.

**ST:** Didn't the Dead start recording their first album in the beginning of 1967?

**MG:** In early 1967 they went down to L.A. and I went with them. They were taking my diet pills at the time and that's why there are accelerated tempos on that album. That was their first experience in the studio. Their producer was this typical L.A. guy, with jowls, heavy tan, long slicked-back hair, lots of Vitalis, white cardigan sweater with a gold wrist watch. They couldn't handle Dave Hassinger at all but he was trying to be cool and they were giving him a hard time. He'd make suggestions and they would say stuff like, "It'll ruin everything if we do it that way." The album came out and it's my favorite album and will always be my favorite because that is the time Jerry and I got together and started living together. We stayed at the Tropicana Motel in Los Angeles during that time.

**ST:** Who did the cover on the first album?

**MG:** That was a collage by a friend of ours — Kelley — who is a meticulous craftsman. The photograph on the back is one of my all-time favorites. It was on the stairs of our house, a typical scene on the stairs. The poster artists, Kelley, Mouse, Rick Griffin, and Wes Wilson were a big part of our early scene.

**ST:** What was Jerry like back then?

**MG:** Jerry would practice six or seven hours a day. The guy was clearly an obsessive.

**ST:** How did you like that?

**MG:** I thought it was great. He was the hardest working person I knew, since in those days there were distractions aplenty in San Francisco. There was a lot going on in the city.

**ST:** It was the beginning of the Summer of Love.

**MG:** Right. All kinds of hip stuff was happening. There were the Diggers who had a place together near our house they called the Free Store. The first anybody had zoned in on the energy of something being free. That was the beginning of the free energy. There was a couple of little head stands down the street. These two brothers who ran the psychedelic shop were good friends and came up to the house often. We'd have great scenes out there in the morning. The sun would shine and we'd all sit out there on the steps and the fog would pour out. We'd talk and talk and smoke joints and have a good time.

I remember Weir at that time was a strict vegetarian and he had gone completely macrobiotic and was very gourmet. He had his own trip in the kitchen. He had his own cupboard, Japanese food, weird stuff. He was making himself macrobiotic muffins that were like cannonballs. You had to attack them with a hammer, but they tasted good.

JIM MARSHALL

**ST:** It's amazing that these five guys got together and developed this unique music.

**MG:** They had a rehearsal studio at the Heliport in Sausalito. They'd commute to Sausalito and rehearse at this place. They did that faithfully. They'd rehearse five days a week, no matter what, unless they were on the road. Jerry insisted on it, and so did Phil. They wanted it to be good, they really did.

GENE ANTHONY

**ST:** Did you travel with the band?

**MG:** In those days we went everywhere together.

**ST:** Did you go to New York with the band when they went there for the first time in June 1967?

**MG:** Yes. I remember when they played the Cafe Au Go-Go. What a scene it was, getting the equipment in. The Cafe Au Go-Go was a real small place and by this time the Grateful Dead had distinguished themselves by having an inordinate amount of equipment because of the Bear.

**ST:** When did the Bear get involved?

**MG:** Bear was involved at the beginning. He was already involved at the Hell's Angels weekend in La Honda. He supplied a lot of energy that we needed, an eerie symbiosis. He helped them out endlessly, but things had to be done his way. Sound checks could be an eight-hour mindbender. They liked what he did, but he was extremely demanding and he finally split the scene.

Janis Joplin at Monterey Pop Festival

**ST:** Wasn't the Monterey Pop Festival also in June 1967?

**MG:** That was a great scene. That was my first look at Jimi Hendrix. Nobody had seen him before on the West Coast. It was nuts! Janis Joplin was fabulous too, and Ravi Shankar.

**ST:** How come the Dead weren't in the movie *Monterey Pop*?

**MG:** The Dead were having equipment problems at the show and weren't happy with their performance; that's why they weren't in the movie. Janis and Jimi were cosmic enough for everybody. They were totally into it. They put themselves totally on the line at that show. Then Otis Redding came on and topped it all off.

**Jimi Hendrix at Monterey Pop Festival**

**ST:** What was it like when Mickey joined the band in the fall of 1967?

**MG:** Mickey joined the band when they were playing at the Straight Theatre. He had been giving Kreutzmann drumming lessons and one day they asked him to come play a set with the band. It sounded incredible with two drummers. It added this fourth dimension to the band that was really a knockout. Everybody went crazy. He added a lot of sound to the band. He has a lot of energy and was a good shot in the arm for them.

**ST:** How did the band react after they would play a hot show?

**MG:** They'd be really up after a good show. They would sit around and talk and rave for hours. They'd be really happy about it. The band would play for all those hours and then be barely able to move. For 15 or 20 minutes they would just sit back. You'd hand them a joint or something cold to drink and they would just be rubber. They'd realize they had played really great and get real high from it and feel that way until the next day.

**ST:** Whose idea was it to play Haight Street in March of 1968?

**MG:** It started early in the morning and I think it was Rock's idea. The band kept saying, maybe we can do it, maybe we can't, all the way up to the wire. There were two flatbed trucks end to end across the street about two blocks down from the park, on Haight Street. They played during the day and everybody we knew was there. It was great to see the street full of people. It was the flowering of that type of event. The city had just started closing the street on weekends and making it a mall and it was a big block party. So the street was closed to traffic and, instead, packed with people. It was beautiful.

**ST:** What happened to change Haight-Ashbury?

**MG:** After *Time* magazine came out with that article on Haight-Ashbury, it filled up with people from all over the country and the atmosphere changed very fast. When the Grateful Dead played on Haight Street it was an incredible experience, but it was the culmination of that free era.

**ST:** What was the Carousel Ballroom like?

**MG:** It was a beautiful place; nobody could believe it. It had wooden floors, a fairly low ceiling, plus sets of French doors that opened to let in fresh air. It also had beautiful gold framed mirrors, strange '50s light fixtures, weird old tables, and red plush sofas. It even had a great kitchen and we served dinner too.

**ST:** So the Carousel was a magical place?

**MG:** It was great. We'd have dinner and a concert for some ridiculously low price, serving really righteous food, a big dining-room scene in this huge old ballroom.

**ST:** Was there any night at the Carousel that stands out in your mind?

**MG:** I remember one time where everybody dosed this one jug of apple juice. There were five or six distributors in the room and each one put something in it, thinking it was clean when they got it. So it got to the point where two swallows was a serious dose. I took one little sip and instantly knew it was electric. Nobody knew how electric it really was. That was the famous night of the lobster claws in the sky and the pterodactyls in the garden. I slithered home across the Golden Gate Bridge in my car at about 5 mph, and I'm still not sure how I did it. Robert Hunter woke up in the street the next morning and had no idea how he got there. That was my last acid trip for a long time and the last for a lot of others too!

**ST:** Any comments about "Dark Star?"

**MG:** It was an excuse for the band to get really weird with a lot of feedback and harmonics and stuff. They'd usually only play "Dark Star" if they were pretty high. It was frequently the peak of the concert when they played "Dark Star." It could be a wonderfully harmonious experience or it could sound like a subway collision at high speed.

## CHET HELMS

Chet Helms ran Family Dog Productions, which produced weekly concerts in San Francisco for several years beginning in 1966. He was a close friend of Janis Joplin and he brought her to San Francisco from Texas to sing in the band he was managing at the time, Big Brother and the Holding Company. Helms was an integral part of the San Francisco music scene.

**ST:** Could you give me some background information about how you got involved in the San Francisco music scene?

**CH:** I graduated from high school in Fort Worth, Texas, in 1960 and went to the University of Texas at Austin. I became involved there with a folk music club. One of my pleasures was to go to the student union building on Friday nights and listen to folk singers there. Also, because of that connection with the folk music group, in 1962 I met David Freiberg and Sandy Rudin who were folk singers for peace. They had been hitchhiking around the world, nonprofit, singing peace songs and trying to stimulate interest in the peace movement.

I was very involved with the peace movement and also the civil rights movement. We were actively picketing theaters across the street from the University of Texas at that time that would not allow blacks in them even though certain class assignments were made that required all students to watch certain movies. Black kids could get in the university but they couldn't see the movies with us because they were in segregated theaters across the street from the campus. I went to college as a young Republican and came out as a young Democrat, actually a YPSL (Young Peoples Socialist Leaguer).

I came to California in 1962 to go to Sandy Rudin's wedding. California was the halcyon world, and I had this dream of moving back to California because I was born there. I dropped out of the university in my second year and went to San Francisco. The day I arrived there was a big peace demonstration protesting nuclear testing in the Pacific, and it had been organized by Ira Sandperl and Joan Baez. So for the first eight days I was in San Francisco, I slept on the pavement in a sleeping bag. David Freiberg was hanging out there with Michaela. David and Michaela were a folk duo at that time.

I met a lot of interesting people who later were influential to me. I met Tony Serra, a lawyer who was involved with liberal progressive causes. After the first eight days David Freiberg, who had an apartment on Central in Haight-Ashbury, let me crash there for six months or so. San Francisco was a real party town throughout the early '60s period and there was an extensive party circuit of people who were associated. It was usual on any given weekend to go to ten or fifteen parties. People sort of traveled in groups.

In 1963 I ended up hitching back to Austin. I met Janis Joplin in the folk music scene back there. There was an apartment house in Austin, referred to as "The Ghetto," where the bohemian students lived because of the low rent. It was basically full of crash pads with eight or nine people sleeping on the floor. There was lots of music, people sitting around singing songs, writing songs, drinking, and smoking tobacco. There wasn't much pot around at that point. I met Janis there and she was unlike any woman I had met in Texas. This was an era when the University of Texas coeds wore a grey-wool sheath skirt, white bobby socks, penny loafers, white blouse, and hair done in a B-52 or beehive.

Janis wore blue jeans, work shirts, and no bra at a time when that was pretty radical, and swore like a sailor. I would comment that I always felt that was an act on Janis' part. Janis was actually one of the better educated and more literate people that I knew. She read voraciously for the whole time I knew her. Whether she was involved in the music business or drugged out or whatever was happening, she read constantly. She had a huge library and was an extremely well-read person and ultimately ended up about one course shy of a degree in history at the University of Texas.

Janis was part of the folk music crowd but she was fundamentally fairly shy, and you had to get her pretty drunk or she wouldn't sing at all. I was into the beat poetry scene and I had long hair and a beard. Janis had spent a summer in Venice in 1961 and so she had an affinity for that image. Here she was in college and I was hitching around the country writing and reading poetry, which had great romantic appeal for her. Joan Baez was big at that time and folk was where it was at, but the delivery of folk music on the West Coast was very slick and polished. When I first heard Janis I thought that if people in California heard Janis it would knock their socks off. I talked to Janis a lot about California and what was happening in San Francisco. We were kind of the beatnik crowd at the university.

Janis and I talked about what was happening on the West Coast and what was happening in the folk music scene there, so she ended up dropping out of school and she and I hitchhiked to Fort Worth to my mother's house. My mother was a fundamentalist Christian teetotaler all of her life, daughter of a Baptist minister. We got to Fort Worth and Janis is there in blue jeans, a work shirt, and no bra, and is saying let's go get some beer, let's party. My mother was fairly polite and when it came time to go to sleep I figured we would stay there since Janis and I weren't sleeping together, but my mother didn't see it that way, so there was a big fight and my brother ended up taking Janis and me to the edge of Fort Worth and depositing us on the road in the middle of the night. We hitchhiked to San Francisco in about fifty hours.

Janis was never more feminine than at that particular time. She was frightened on the road and was as feminine as I had ever experienced her. We ended up in San Francisco and crashed on David Freiberg's floor, and also at 1090 Page Street.

We actually were only together for a couple of months before we went our own way. The first day we got to San Francisco we were prowling around North Beach. The only place I could find for her to play was at the Coffee and Confusion, which was run by an older beatnik named Sylvia. The owner had a house policy that on Monday Night hootenanny all the performances were free and you couldn't pass the hat or be paid. Janis had her autoharp. Janis was a different Janis vocally at that time.

She would do "Stealin'" and some of the traditional country blues songs that have a gospel orientation. Janis sang that night unaccompanied other than strumming her autoharp and belted out these country blues songs and got a standing ovation so that the owner wanted to have her back. Janis was so good that she overcame the house policy and the owner let the hat be passed around, and hired her to perform at the coffeehouse on other occasions for about fifty dollars a night. That doesn't sound like a lot of money now but it was a lot back then. Then she played at the Coffee Gallery and places down in Palo Alto like Saint Michael's Alley. Jerry Garcia and Jorma Kaukonen were down there. That is where she met that crowd of people. During that period she got off into drugs and she and I weren't getting along too well but we stayed in contact.

Also during that time she had two great opportunities that came along to sign a record contract that got side-tracked because she was in an accident on her motor scooter and another time she was mugged by a group of drunks. Janis got off into drugs as early as mid-1964. All her friends were so afraid for her that we bought her a plane ticket to send her back to Texas. We had a big bash and then sent her back to Port Arthur. I lost track of her for a couple of years until I got involved in the music scene with Big Brother and the Holding Company.

With the advent of the Beatles and Rolling Stones, all of us politicos thought there was a breakthrough. It was like you can get the messages across, there's a way to say it, and they can't shut you down.

By this time I'm hanging out at 1090 Page Street, which was managed by Rodney Albin, Peter Albin's brother, the bass player for Big Brother. Rodney ran this big old rooming house, which at one time had been a private family mansion. It had a ballroom in the basement with various accoutrements, and many, many rooms. It was a beautiful old Victorian house. There were a lot of people hanging out there and we got to talking about doing message music like these other groups were doing. We all had political agendas that we wanted to get across, and we had been very frustrated in getting our messages out. Here was the light at the end of the tunnel, the way to get the message out. So Christopher Newton, who is the son of Dwight Newton the TV critic in San Francisco, and myself, and Peter Kramer, who was in Sopwith Camel, Mark Udey, and several other people assembled with the purpose of starting a political message band.

We met at 408 Ashbury and had several meetings and all decided to get a band together. It was really a rhythm section because out of the eight or nine people that were assembling, there were only two that were really musicians. After three or four meetings it kind of dissolved but I still wanted to do it. I wanted to get into a situation where I was with more musicians. Christopher Newton said that there was this old ballroom in the basement of 1090 Page Street. So we went down and talked to Rodney and Peter and for twenty dollars we got the use of the ballroom to do jam sessions. The ballroom held about two hundred people with a stage. It had old wood paneling and stained-glass lamps.

There was no live music scene happening in San Francisco at that time. The folk scene had gone out and there was a real dearth of live music. The few jazz places were tiny and kind of on the downswing, or too expensive. I ended up starting these jam sessions. At the first jam session there were thirty musicians and five spectators. We held about ten of these jam sessions every Tuesday night. Within the first couple of jam sessions that ratio had changed so that there were seven or eight musicians and thirty or forty spectators. By the fourth or fifth one, there were two hundred people watching, and it was a freebie so we thought we had to get control of this because people were smoking pot in the open and under-age kids were drinking alcohol, and we were real paranoid about getting busted. So, at that stage of the game, we decided to charge fifty cents admission and it was our idea to discourage people from coming, not to make money. It got to be too live a party scene. The audience was getting rowdier.

Sam Andrews, Chuck Jones, Peter Albin, and Paul Ferrez became the guys that played together all the time, and it became obvious that these guys were the core unit and so Paul Ferrez asked these guys to form a band called Blue Yard Hill, and I had also asked Peter essentially the same thing. They played a couple of parties as Blue Yard Hill and then I became the manager but nobody liked the name of the band. We had a brainstorming session to figure out a name for the band instead of Blue Yard Hill. Sam Andrews and James Gurley were there. As I recall, James Gurley had been added to the band by then. He had come fresh from Detroit to be with his friends, Luria Castell and Ellen Harmon, who later started the Family Dog. They knew about the jam sessions we were having and brought James to meet Blue Yard Hill at one of the jam sessions at 1090 Page Street.

We ended up taking him on as the lead guitarist in the band. At the brainstorming session after going through various names, maybe twenty names or so, we came up with Big Brother and the Holding Company. There ensued a big argument that it was too long and wouldn't fit on a 45 record but we finally agreed to use it because we didn't like the name Blue Yard Hill. Within two weeks of using the name Big Brother and the Holding Company we were in a national magazine article on West Coast bands with crazy names.

Literally, after a couple of weeks of adopting the name, we had national publicity. The band consisted of Chuck Jones, who was replaced by Dave Getz a short time later, James Gurley on lead guitar, Peter Albin, and Sam Andrews. The name had a lot of double entendres: Big Brother is watching you; the Holding Company as a corporate entity had drug implications and some sinister overtones. The band used to refer to itself as Big Breather and the Holding Nose.

We played a couple of gigs in 1965 at the Open Theatre, which was a real radical free-form improvisatory theatre in Berkeley. We played a couple of gigs there with light shows, which was a very early use of light shows. There was a strobe with abstract expressionist slides being flicked through the projector on the screen. The first rock posters that I can recall other than the Red Dog Saloon were the two that Wes Wilson and I did for Big Brother at the Open Theatre. One was the swami on a bed of nails. Then we did the Trips Festival in January of 1966.

ST: How did you meet the Grateful Dead?

CH: I had known Phil Lesh when he was involved with the San Francisco Mime Troupe. I was good friends with Phil at that time but in a totally non-music context. Phil lived fairly close to 1090 Page Street so we would hang out and talk. I used to go over to a place he lived at on Haight and Broderick and hang out with him. We smoked grass and talked politics, not so much music, because Phil was just getting involved with the Warlocks. He told me that he was going to form this band called the Warlocks with some guys down on the Peninsula that he knew. Phil started talking about this band, and how he liked the name the Warlocks. I didn't know Jerry at that time. In the fall of 1965 they played at the Mime Troupe Benefit. There were two benefits for the Mime Troupe. One was in a warehouse downtown organized by Bill Graham, who was the producer of the Mime Troupe at the time.

The second one was at the Fillmore Auditorium, which featured the Grateful Dead, the Jefferson Airplane, John Handy, and some other groups, as I recall.

ST: That was the first show after the Warlocks changed their name to the Grateful Dead.

CH: That is where I met Bill Graham for the first time. I was introduced to him by my friend, John Carpenter, who managed The Great Society. John and I had been talking about doing a show with his band and the band I managed, Big Brother. The original Family Dog people, Alton Kelly, Ellen Harmon, Luria Castell, and Jack Towle, had done three shows at the Longshoremen's Hall all of which were successful critically but not economically. The Family Dog then did a couple of other shows at California Hall that Rock Scully and Danny Rifkin were involved in. The Family Dog had fundamentally gone bust so Luria, the remaining member, John Carpenter, and I had agreed to doing some shows at the California Hall under the name Family Dog. Luria left for Mexico unexpectedly without confirming the dates for the venue, which left John Carpenter and I in a great quandary as we had already made several commitments to various bands for those dates. John and I attended the Mime Troupe Benefit at the Fillmore. During a meeting with Bill Graham, John Carpenter, and I discussed with him the possibility of doing some shows for the Mime Troupe. Graham said that he was thinking of taking out a lease on the Fillmore Auditorium but was concerned about booking shows every weekend. We then suggested that he fill this need with the previous booking commitments, which we were unable to fulfill at California Hall. At that meeting, Graham decided to take a lease on the Fillmore Auditorium and he would do shows on one weekend and we would do shows on alternate weekends, and we would help him with his shows as well. Graham was not in touch with Haight-Ashbury at the time and was not in touch with the musicians. John and I were street people who knew the musician crowd. On a handshake we agreed to do alternate weekends at the Fillmore.

The first concert was on February 19, 1966 with the Jefferson Airplane and Big Brother. We ended up doing only four shows at the Fillmore Auditorium. We were supposed to do more than that but Graham started to take the weekends we were supposed to have. His shows were billed as Bill Graham Presents and ours were Family Dog shows. In April of 1966 we took the Family Dog shows to the Avalon Ballroom and did the Blues Project and the Great Society. That was our first color poster, by the way. Once we had a hall of our own we started doing shows every weekend.

ST: When did Janis Joplin join Big Brother and the Holding Company?

CH: After Big Brother started getting some notoriety, the band and I discussed getting a vocalist. We started auditioning vocalists. After we had exhausted the supply of available vocalists, I decided to get in touch with Janis to see if she wanted to audition. Janis agreed to do it and dropped out of her last semester in college to come to San Francisco. Janis came out and rehearsed with Big Brother and we knew it was going to work.

We continued rehearsing for a few months after that and by that time Janis became a hot item. Albert Grossman and others were trying to sign her and were courting Janis very heavily. It was at that point that the band and I parted company. Big Brother ended up signing with Bobby Shad of Mainstream Records, against my advice. It ended up being a bad deal for them.

ST: Were the San Francisco bands like the Grateful Dead, the Jefferson Airplane, Quicksilver Messenger Service, and Big Brother a close-knit community in 1966?

CH: At that point there was a coming together of the community and the recognition that the groups were into the same things. Improvisation was a general characteristic of them all. The San Francisco environment permitted experimentation and improvisation. The fusion of musical traditions was a part of it. I think that Ravi Shankar was an influence. He was already a cult figure in Haight-Ashbury at that time. His long, extended improvisational solos were an influence. Also the jazz tradition of improvisation had an impact.

ST: You put on many shows featuring the San Francisco bands.

CH: Quicksilver and Big Brother were virtually house bands with us. Quicksilver played their first gig for me and they played many of their subsequent gigs for me, more so than Graham. The Dead and the Airplane played there quite often. The first time the Grateful Dead played was on May 28, 1966 and they were the opening band on the bill for the Grassroots and the Leaves.

ST: What was the Avalon Ballroom like?

CH: It held about 1,200 people and was located at 1268 Sutter Street at Van Ness. The ballroom was upstairs above a storefront in a building, which was built in 1911 as a dance academy, and it had been part of the Avalon chain of ballrooms in the thirties. The inside was a classic ballroom with a row of balconies around the top, sort of booths or boxes that were ornate and gilded. It had gilded columns, gilded mirrors, red-flock raised wallpaper, a room with a fireplace. The upstairs had a full bar setup where we served food but no alcohol. There was a puppet stage upstairs that was a duplicate of the ballroom and mirrored it. There were many diversionary areas for people to get into: There was the light show, the strobe you could stand under, black lights, huge sheets of fluorescent paper which people tore up and made into elaborate designs. We had chalks for people to paint their face with, and areas where you could sit down. There were a number of environments that people could go into; they didn't have to be locked into just looking at the stage all the time. There was an open dance floor and the room had great acoustics because it had an acoustically draped ceiling.

**ST:** What were the light shows like at the Avalon?

**CH:** I chose not to go with one light show. At the shows at the Fillmore we used Tony Martin, who was a hangover from the Trips Festival. The screens were still up from the Fillmore Acid Test and The Trips Festival so Graham and I used Tony Martin at the Fillmore. When I went to the Avalon I used Bill Ham, Ben Van Meter, and a variety of other light shows. I used different people to spice up the light shows for variety. I liked to have a venue where a variety of artists could be seen.

**ST:** Could you describe the light shows?

**CH:** What was unique about the San Francisco light shows was the intimate coordination with the music, the fact that it was a performance that was rhythmic and coordinated with the music, virtually a harmonic on the music, as opposed to being simply colorful lights going on in the background. A gentleman named Seymour Locke who was a professor at San Francisco State University had been reading about Stravinsky's experiments with lights and light shows in the teens and twenties when he did the "Rites of Spring." Stravinsky had done light shows in the teens and twenties, so Seymour Locke did extensive studies of these early light shows and he came up with the idea of the liquid lights using an overhead projector and liquids of varying solvencies that would mix or not mix depending on how they were put together. Locke taught Tony Martin, Bill Ham, and Elias Romero (who was involved with the San Francisco Tape Music Center) about liquid lights. Elias Romero and Bill Ham did a number of shows together, and Tony Martin did a number of his own at the San Francisco Tape Music Center at 321 Divisadero, in conjunction with other events that were going on there.

There were essentially three traditions locally in San Francisco: there were people who came from the Tony Martin branch that saw the Trips Festival, which had liquid lights in it but had very static elements in it also; then there were people like Ben Van Meter, Jerry Abrams, and Bruce Conner, who were straight out of film tradition using pastiched clips of films, for example; and then there were the ones that were out of the Seymour Locke, Elias Romero, Bill Ham tradition of pure liquid lights. Later there were the computerized light shows.

**ST:** Could you comment about how the psychedelic poster art came about?

**CH:** It arose out of a climate not unlike the great poster era in late nineteenth-century France with Toulouse-Lautrec, which started as event posters too and became fine art. I take some credit for the proliferation of the posters because I employed many different artists to do posters for me. The principal artists identified with that era like Alton Kelley, Stanley Mouse, Victor Moscoso, Rick Griffin, Wes Wilson, and Bob Schnepf got their start with us. Within a very short time after Wes Wilson had started working for me, Graham got an exclusive contract with him to do posters for him. I could have been complacent and gotten a house poster artist like Graham did for a while, but I liked the idea of making it a venue for a variety of artists right from the beginning. So, about the time Wilson left and we did the first poster with Mouse and Kelley, the policy of using different artists was implemented. I should note that at the beginning the first posters were suggested by me in that I would pick the theme of the dance, the central graphic image of the poster, and then give the copy and the information to the artist who would execute the poster. As the Family Dog reached its full stride after several months, I was too busy to continue doing that and the artists did it themselves.

**ST:** The poster from the Grateful Dead concert at the Avalon on September 16-17, 1966 featuring the skull and roses has become a Grateful Dead icon.

**CH:** That was originally an illustration by Sullivan, from *The Rubaiyat of Omar Khayyam* which was originally a black-and-white illustration that was done in the nineteenth century. Kelley and Mouse added the lettering and the color to it.

**ST:** How many posters would you print?

**CH:** Because of economic considerations, the initial poster runs were only three hundred. We would post them around town and people started to take them down and collect them. After about the first year we started to reproduce them for sale.

**ST:** What was the Trips Festival like?

**CH:** The core of it was Zach Stewart and Stewart Brand who were partners in the America Needs Indians Sensorium. It was a sensorium where they set up tepees and a 360-

ever did, but what is important about it is the experimentation that goes on. There was a climate of freedom and permission to do just about anything that didn't hurt somebody.

The most significant thing I read about the '60s was: "There is no such thing as the generation gap; there is but the absence of rites of passage." What the ballrooms were about was a sanctuary, a safe place for evolving rites of passage that fit our lives, our dreams, and our ideals. We were finding new ways to be adult without being militarized or having babies, new ways to achieve maturity, and we were creating our own institutions to affirm and accept those ways. We wanted to create environments in which there was a marketplace of ideas, where things could be sorted out, a variety of things tried in a safe situation.

**ST:** What was the Grateful Dead house at 710 Ashbury Street like?

**CH:** It had about fifteen rooms including closets, which in those days were used as bedrooms. People would crash there at times. I stayed there on a few occasions. People would drop acid and sit around philosophizing about the world.

**ST:** Any good stories about the Monterey Pop Festival?

**CH:** I was on my way into the Monterey Pop Festival in a friend's car and Jimi Hendrix was walking along the road outside the gate, with his guitar case, headed into the fairgrounds. I had met Jimi Hendrix in England in January of 1967 when he was virtually unknown and was hanging around the Marquis Club. We hit it off because we were both Americans floating through the English scene. Anyway, we stopped, and gave him a ride, and he and I exchanged hellos, and then proceeded into the festival. The last night of Monterey Pop everyone took a lot of Owsley acid. There were big gallon jars of Monterey Pop Festival Purple going around, and you could dip your hand in and take a fistful out and stick them in your pocket, and it was being passed out to the crowd and being taken by everyone.

My partner at that time was Bob Cohen and we did the free stage at Monterey Pop, which was at Monterey Peninsula College. He and I organized the truck and organized the bands. Virtually everyone who played on the main stage played in some configuration on the free stage: members of the Dead, the Airplane, Quicksilver, Janis Joplin, and Hendrix. After the shows had ended some of the musicians had a jam session. One jam involved Jimi Hendrix on guitar and David Freiberg on bass, and they played for several hours. We were all totally out of our minds on acid and it was wonderful. The next morning we are all crashed out on the lawn in a dazed state, still pretty stoned on acid. I realized that I had to get a ride back to San Francisco. My ride had already left the night before.

There was an old van that belonged to Stanley Mouse that he had left behind with Bob Seidemann. Mouse had already gone back to the city. Seidemann was the Dead's photographer, and he had Mouse's van, which was loaded with demonstration equipment that Fender Guitar Company had loaned for free to the Grateful Dead for use by the bands at the festival. After the festival, Rock Scully and Danny Rifkin got the equipment to use for concerts in the Panhandle.

So Seidemann has this van and I hitched a ride with him and Joanne, a light show artist who also needed a ride. Meantime, we are still stoned out of our minds on acid and we leave the festival and we are out on the highway outside of Monterey and we get pulled over by the CHP. The cop comes up and he smiles and asks for the registration, and immediately Seidemann starts giggling and says, "Officer you're not going to believe this, but this van belongs to a friend of mine and I don't have it." Then the officer asks for Seidemann's driver's license, and Seidemann again starts giggling and says, "Officer, you're not going to believe this, but I don't have it." The whole time the three of us are in hysterics, giggling and laughing because we are on acid, and pretty soon the cop is into the same giggling and laughing thing too. Everything he asked us we replied, "Officer, you're not going to believe this but" or some excuse and it was so absurd that we started laughing hysterically. Eventually he let us go but he wrote a 21 item fix-it ticket for no tail lights, a broken door, you name it. The cop ended up being a real nice guy and letting us go after he told us to take it easy going home. We eventually got back to San Francisco. The equipment did get used in the Panhandle a few times before it was returned to Fender.

More than a year later Hendrix is back in San Francisco and he calls me and asks me to put together a jam with him and Quicksilver and the Grateful Dead. He said he really enjoyed jamming with Freiberg at Monterey and would like to do it again with Quicksilver and the Grateful Dead. He asked me to set it up for him. I told him, "Sure, I think I can set it up," so I made a few calls and got it together. A friend of mine was managing this restaurant in Sausalito that was on a ferry boat and I set it up for Quicksilver and the Dead to show up and jam with Hendrix. That weekend the Dead were playing for me at the Avalon and they had already played at least one night when Hendrix called the following day and wanted to jam with them. I called Hendrix back and told him to meet us at the ferry boat in Sausalito at 2:00 a.m., that the Dead and Quicksilver would be there and we would jam all night. After the Dead's gig we go out to this place, and the guys in the Dead are beat and dead-tired because they had just played the Avalon, but after all it's a jam with Hendrix, who was a hot item. We sit there from 2:00 a.m. until morning and Hendrix never shows. Everybody in Quicksilver and the Dead were pissed.

The Dead played again at the Avalon that night and Hendrix shows up there while the Dead are playing. Hendrix comes up to me and I told him that the Grateful Dead and Quicksilver and I were waiting for him all night in Sausalito, and I asked him what happened. Hendrix says, "Oh, I met this broad and we dropped acid and we fucked all night," and I said, "That's great but you should have let us know, you had ten guys sitting there all night who were dead-tired, waiting to jam with you because you asked for it." Hendrix said, "Can I jam with the Grateful Dead tonight on the stage?" and I said, "It's okay with me, but it's their gig, it's their show, if they want that to happen, it's fine with me."

At that point I was already having problems with the permit authorities for the ballroom and there was a curfew of midnight which was strictly enforced, but which the Dead willingly complied with. I brought Hendrix into the dressing room and told the Dead that Jimi wanted to jam with them, and they're saying, "Great, we'll do it." The Grateful Dead go back out on stage to do their last set of the night and start playing, and keep playing. I tell Hendrix and everybody that no matter what happens I'm pulling the plug at midnight. What happened was the Dead kept playing and kept telling him to wait, and played out their set. At about 11:45 when Hendrix realizes that he isn't going to get to play he comes to me and I said, "Look, you stood up ten people last night at this jam you set up, I don't blame them if they don't want to play with you. It's fine with me but I told you it was up to them, and they obviously don't want to do it." So Hendrix never jammed with the Grateful Dead, and the bottom line is they were pissed at him. The Grateful Dead played a good set, and had a good weekend other than they were deprived of sleep.

MICHAEL ZAGARIS

## ROCK SCULLY

Rock Scully is a close friend of Jerry Garcia and a former manager of the Grateful Dead. Scully was a moving force in the early Dead scene and helped the band gain national recognition.

**ST:** Rock, could you tell me how you became manager of the Grateful Dead?

**RS:** I was a graduate student at San Francisco State College and there was a group of us at State College that were living in Haight-Ashbury and we were promoting concerts under the name Family Dog. This was before Chet Helms took it over. Ken Kesey was lecturing around the Bay Area at that time and I went and saw him. Owsley had also shown up at the lecture and he told me about this band the Grateful Dead. I went to an Acid Test down on the Peninsula and heard them and thought they were great. A few days later Owsley asked me if I wanted to manage them. Since I had experience with promoting concerts with the Family Dog they figured I would be good at getting them work. I hooked up with them and started getting them work and shaping their career. We went down to Los Angeles to woodshed — to rehearse the music, write some new tunes, develop a new set. We rented a big old house on the fringes of Watts that at one time had been an expensive home. We filled it up with rock and roll gear and started practicing. Danny Rifkin and I ran around Los Angeles setting up dance concerts so the band could get exposure and keep playing in front of people. When we returned to San Francisco the band moved into 710 Ashbury Street.

**ST:** Was the Acid Test where you first saw the Dead play the Big Beat Acid Test?

**RS:** Yes, it was at a place called the Beat Club down near the highway in Palo Alto. Kesey had the Grateful Dead set up at one end of the room, and he had his band set up at the other end of the room. In the middle was a tower full of light show gear, speakers, microphones, and slide projectors. Stewart Brand was there and he had his *America Needs Indians* show, which he was projecting up on a sheet on the wall. There were sheets down at either end of the room with liquid projections, slides, and movies. It was a bizarre out-of-control scene. Cassady was there doing his thing.

**ST:** What was Cassady like?

**RS:** I would liken him to a poet. He was always spouting off quotes from his most recent reading. He did it in a musical way with the rest of the room in mind even if no one was listening. He would also juggle with the sounds of the room and with what other people were doing. He could have several things going on at the same time. He was very off the cuff and very avant-garde. He was a day ahead in any conversation. He never forgot a road he had driven. He could go through these amazing turns and look at you and never look at the road. He had feelings and eyes in back of his head.

ST: That explains why he was the driver of the Prankster bus.

RS: He was also the driver in Kerouac's book *On the Road*. He was Moriarity. Driving was his specialty. It was amazing because he rarely had his eyes on the road but he was a great driver. Driving was just one of the things he did while he was talking and juggling all kinds of stuff.

ST: What was Kesey's place like up in the hills in La Honda?

RS: Sort of like a big summer retreat. There were speakers hanging in the trees. It was a combination of funk and high tech. Wherever you went out in the woods near the house you could hear people talking in the house and you would hear music playing.

ST: Did the Dead play up in La Honda? I know they played for most of the Acid Tests.

RS: I think they must have played there one time. But most of the time it was rather loose.

ST: How did Owsley get involved with the band?

RS: Owsley was an early financial backer of the band. Owsley put money into getting the band good sound equipment and he was the one who financed the woodshed period in Los Angeles. Owsley provided the money for the concerts we promoted ourselves in Los Angeles at the Troopers Hall and Danish Hall.

ST: Would you say that the notoriety the band had prior to the first album was due to the Acid Tests?

RS: The name they got for themselves started out with the acid tests and the Trips Festival but those were very localized events. The Dead became a community band and the early shows were for the people of the city of San Francisco. But as the hippie scene started to escalate with more and more people coming to Haight-Ashbury word of the band started to spread.

   The hippie scene at that time had something amazing going for it in that it was an international scene full of traveling people. It was a youth movement and a lot of the people had other things going like being artists, writers, and musicians. The hippie scene growing out of the Beat scene was a very mobile scene. People were coming and going from other centers such as Big Sur, Shasta, Eugene, Portland, Seattle, Los Angeles, New York City, London, and Amsterdam. A lot of the people in the hip scene had traveled extensively around the world. The Grateful Dead as a band, however, had never been out of California at that time but the word began to spread. With new people coming into Haight-Ashbury all the time the Dead got a lot of exposure since they were a part of the Haight-Ashbury community. With the two ballrooms that were happening, the Fillmore and Avalon, and the free concerts we were doing in the park and on the street, we did a good job of developing an ever-increasing audience.

**ST:** When did the band move into 710 Ashbury Street?

**RS:** That was in 1966. I was living at 710 with Danny Rifkin and it was a boarding house. Danny had an apartment downstairs and I had a bedroom upstairs. When the band returned to San Francisco after I took them to the woodshed in Los Angeles they needed a place to stay so Danny moved some people out of the boarding house and the band moved in.

GENE ANTHONY

710 Ashbury

**ST:** The house at 710 became a focal point for a lot of activity.

**RS:** It was sort of a community center. It got so busy that we had to take over 715 across the street. It was almost impossible to get any business done there. We had the Grateful Dead offices in the front room downstairs, and most of the band lived there except Phil and Billy. That house was jammed packed all the time. People were stopping by, the front steps were always crowded with people. The whole neighborhood was very social that way. Janis and Big Brother lived down the street. The Charlatans lived in the neighborhood. The Airplane and Quicksilver would always stop by. Our house became a center of activity and there was always something going on.

The Grateful Dead, the Jefferson Airplane, Quicksilver Messenger Service, Janis Joplin & Big Brother & the Holding Company, & the Charlatans on the Doorsteps of 710 Ashbury

stop and take notice. They would even take them down and collect them. Putting the posters out helped spread the word.

ST: The music that the Dead, Quicksilver, and the Airplane performed at concerts beginning in 1966 included long instrumental pieces.

RS: That's because those early concerts were dance concerts and the dancers didn't want the songs to end. Dancing was a real important part of it and the band wasn't always the focus of attention. The band was literally playing to their audience. That was the form that kind of took off when the psychedelic hippie thing spread out of San Francisco. Our next available venues across the country were dance halls. People who had seen us in San Francisco would want to export us to their towns. Slowly but surely there were places for us to travel to and play at.

To tell you the truth the scene in Haight-Ashbury in 1966 was really not that big until the media got a hold of it and then it became huge. Events like the Human Be-In and the Monterey Pop Festival focused a lot of attention on the hippie scene in northern California. People from all across the nation started emulating the hippie scene in Haight-Ashbury, and consequently the demand for us started to grow.

ST: With the ballroom scene happening, it seemed like the band was playing almost every weekend.

RS: The demand was there to play, but I was worried that we were going to overdo it. We desperately needed to get out of San Francisco so we booked our first shows in New York.

ST: What was it like bringing the band to New York for the first time in 1967?

RS: It was one of those things where we had to work hard and work our way up. The band was totally unlike anything New York style. We did those free concerts in Tompkins Square Park and Central Park because it was a good way to expose the band and get the word out about them.

ST: What was it like when the Dead ventured out of California and they were perceived as the Haight-Ashbury hippie band spreading the message of peace and love?

RS: Though at times we felt like the messenger it was tough on the band because the Grateful Dead were just a band of musicians who didn't mean to be proponents of any movement. At best they were representative of San Francisco's music scene, and never meant to be in the vanguard of any youth movement. One of the hardest jobs I had was to keep the record company from advertising us as a hippie band who were harbingers of peace, love, and flower power representing the hippie movement. Especially after the Monterey Pop Festival promoters wanted to sell us that way. Though we considered ourselves hippies we weren't the hippie movement. We were musicians first, and we had enough to hang on to with the music. We wanted to be recognized as musicians. My problem was with the press who wanted to write about us as a sociological movement rather than as musicians. Our involvement in the movement was as entertainers, the musicians who were willing to take risks musically. We didn't want to take a political stance, though it was risky politically in the United States to be an avowed taker of LSD and smoker of reefer. It wasn't that we were promoting it, we were just users of it. But wherever we went we were always being written up as pot-smoking, LSD-crazed hippies from San Francisco who were part of the hippie movement, and the musician part came last. That was a real problem and the band had to earn their stripes as musicians. Unfortunately the first few albums didn't do that for us.

It wasn't until *Workingman's Dead* and *American Beauty* came out, which were listenable to more of the mainstream, did we start getting the recognition we deserved. The fact is that the Dead are an experiential phenomenon and the concerts are experienced by both the band and the audience and that doesn't translate to a disc real easily. For the Dead to work within the confines of a recording studio is a different ball game, which Jerry has pointed out many times. The hippie movement escalated so fast that there was very little we could do about the press not treating us as musicians and not considering our music, but rather emphasizing the sociological movement that we were a part of. The only answer we could come up with was to keep working on the music.

**ST:**  How would you describe the Monterey Pop Festival in June 1967?

**RS:**  It was fantastic. You see, I come from that area and I know the political people there. For me, it was a lot of local politics because I realized the thing was going to be oversold. So consequently, I helped arrange impromptu jam sessions at the free campground that we organized at Monterey College. We knew there would be overflow so we let people camp there and we set up a stage and after the shows the various bands would put on jam sessions.

**ST:** Who played over there at the college?

**RS:** Jimi Hendrix, Eric Burdon, Jerry Garcia, Phil Lesh, the Airplane. We did that one night over there and then another night at one of the halls where people were camped in on the fairgrounds. So there were two nights of jams. They were fantastic. We even set up light shows.

**ST:** Did the Dead play on the free stage?

**RS:** No, it wasn't the entire Dead. It was Garcia, Phil, and individual musicians from various bands jamming together. At the time we hadn't met some of the musicians. We hadn't met Hendrix and we didn't know the Who. We got to know them there. We all took acid together and played all night. Since Danny and I were doing free concerts up in the Panhandle, there was a sense that we couldn't go wrong. The equipment at the festival was free from Fender, who had just been bought out by CBS. After the festival was over, we managed to get the equipment moved up to San Francisco. With that equipment, we got Hendrix to play at the Panhandle.

**ST:** What other concerts did you put on at the Panhandle?

**RS:** It was always the Grateful Dead or the Dead and Airplane, or Big Brother and Quicksilver ... that sort of thing.

**ST:** The Dead were known for doing free concerts in Haight-Ashbury.

**RS:** It was an outgrowth of a need of the community and since the community was supporting us in the ballrooms it was our way of paying them back. It was a spontaneous gesture on our part and normally we didn't have permits. We'd rent the flatbed trucks and a generator, show up early in the morning, set it up and start playing until the cops shut us down. It was a way of keeping people off the streets and getting them out to the park.

**ST:** You helped write the pursuit of happiness speech, which was read at the press conference after the band had gotten busted at 710 in October 1967. Can you recount how that speech came about?

**RS:** Well, it was just how we felt at the time. We were pissed off that the authorities had screwed with us. We thought we had every right to smoke pot and we just didn't want to be fucked with. We had a feeling that the laws were going to change. We were hoping they would, anyway.

**ST:** What was Haight-Ashbury like in its heyday?

**RS:** It was just beautiful. Everybody was in love with the neighborhood. There were friends everywhere. We knew all the store owners. Everybody really cared for each other and looked after the neighborhood. It was really neat.

**ST:** Did you have anything to do with putting together the Pacific northwest tour in January and February of 1968 . . . the time the band was recording the *Anthem of the Sun* album?

**RS:** Yes. That was the first tour that we undertook with another band from San Francisco. We went with the Quicksilver. The Quick and the Dead Tour we called it. We toured the great Pacific northwest. We booked the gigs ourselves. We

JIM MARSHALL

didn't make much money but it was a load of fun.

**ST:** How did the free show on Haight Street on March 3, 1968 come about?

**RS:** We did that one without a permit. It was a day when the street was closed to traffic. Haight Street had gotten so crowded with bumper-to-bumper traffic that the city closed it to vehicles. We thought it would be perfect to slide our trucks across the street and play. We piled all the equipment on to flatbed trucks and just pulled up in front of the Straight Theatre and plugged in to their electricity. We had two flatbed trucks back to back set up across Haight Street, which we used as our stage. The band played for a couple of hours. The entire length of Haight Street was literally filled up all the way past Divisadero. Immediately the cops were trying to unplug us but we were running off the Straight Theatre and we had that place fortified. The cops couldn't get near the electricity. We were running it right out of the second-floor window so the cops couldn't cut us off. It was an amazing day.

**ST:** Was there an M.C.?

**RS:** Not a word said. In those days when we didn't have permission or permits to play music outdoors, we made sure that nobody could take the blame.

**ST:** How did the Dead get to play at Columbia University in May 1968 during the student strike there?

**RS:** I went down and met with the demonstrators. We struck a deal that they couldn't use our sound system for political announcements if we would come and play for their strike. The whole campus was surrounded by police so the band was smuggled on campus in a bread truck. We went into the building in the bread truck with all our gear and smuggled it up in an elevator and set it up on the student union square.

**ST:** What prompted the band to move out of Haight-Ashbury?

**RS:** Haight-Ashbury was getting too crowded and Gray Line tour buses were going past our house as part of their tour. People were coming by the house at all hours of the night and day, and there was no privacy. Don't get me wrong; a lot of times it was fun because the people who came by were visiting bands like the Who, Eric Burdon and the Animals, the Airplane, but it was hard to take care of business effectively so we bailed and moved to Marin.

**ST:** Where to?

**RS:** First we moved to Camp Lagunitas. Camp Lagunitas was a wonderful place. It had a swimming pool, a cook house, and a dining hall that had a piano in it where the band would play. Janis and Big Brother lived right across the road. Pigpen and Janis were having an affair at the time and it was a lot of fun. Janis would be over singing with us all the time. You could hear Pig and Janis singing in the middle of the night. They were real tight. Pig and Janis sang together on stage a few times too.

**ST:** Isn't Camp Lagunitas where those Indian raids took place?

**RS:** That was fun. Quicksilver lived nearby and we would pretend we were Indians and go out and raid Quicksilver's ranch because they dressed like cowboys. You know, friendly rivalries — kids' stuff.

**ST:** Where did the band live next?

**RS:** After Camp Lagunitas the band moved to Olompali. Olompali was a big old Spanish estate that had a swimming pool, some outbuildings with bedrooms, and enough space so that we all could live there and have a good time. We would

**Janis & Pigpen at the Northern California Folk-Rock Festival, May 18, 1968**

get the word out that we were having a party and people would come and jam. It wasn't a set thing where the Dead would play but it was a jam session where musicians from the Airplane, Quicksilver, the Charlatans would jam with us. It was a chance for all our friends from the city to come and hang out with us outdoors in the sunshine. We'd set up the stage between the house and the pool and people would being doing acid and hanging out by the pool naked. Sometimes there would be several hundred people partying.

**ST:** Didn't the Dead start hanging out with Crosby in Marin?

**RS:** Crosby had been friendly with a lot of the San Francisco musicians from the folk music scene earlier on. He already knew Garcia from that scene but when he moved from L.A. to Marin he became a neighbor of ours and he started hanging out with the guys in the band. Garcia, Lesh, and Weir really enjoyed Crosby, Stills, and Nash harmonies and I think Crosby's influence helped the band improve their harmonies. This led to the tighter format of songs that appeared on *Workingman's Dead* and *American Beauty*. Certainly Garcia and Weir, who had come out of a folk and bluegrass period, knew the vocal harmony trip, and it was a combination of their background in that type of music and knowing the historical roots of American music, which helped evolve those albums. *Workingman's Dead* and *American Beauty* are a reflection of their bluegrass and folk roots.

**ST:** While it is true that *Workingman's Dead* and *American Beauty* were two of the band's best-selling albums, the music on *Anthem of the Sun* and *Live Dead* reflects what the band was playing in the ballrooms.

**RS:** *Workingman's Dead* and *American Beauty* were a breakthrough in that they reached a lot of people that didn't understand the other kinds of music that we played. However, *Anthem of the Sun* and *Live Dead* represent the avant-garde, freeform jazz style of rock music that the band really enjoyed playing. The band got their rocks off playing those long jams because that was the new music. What really excited the band were the machinations that their music took on in those extended jams. The long extended cuts were what enabled the dance concerts to happen. The dancing could get crazy and out of sight and go on and on. So much of the Grateful Dead shows at those dance concerts really had to do with the audience and the Dead very seriously tried to reflect where their audience was at and were very affected by their audience. Their music was very experiential and experimental. "Dark Star" for instance was a song that meandered through an incredible number of changes and no one knew where it would end up, or what song would come out of it or how long it would go. Oftentimes they would play other songs in the middle of it. It would start off in such a bizarre amazing way, and climax, and climax again, and recede into the most quiet music they ever played. It was a ground for very experimental electronic stuff to happen. People loved it for the mystery of it.

**ST:** How did the Garcia-Hunter collaboration come about?
**RS:** Garcia and Hunter met in the early sixties when they were both folk musicians hanging out in Palo Alto near Stanford University. They played in a number of folk and bluegrass

Robert Hunter

bands together. Hunter was a writer and had also experimented with LSD. He was involved in those government experiments at Stanford. Garcia and Hunter began to write tunes together for the Grateful Dead and I think they first appeared on *Aoxomoxoa*. As far as how they go about it, it is my understanding that basically Hunter delivers lyrics and Garcia looks them over and if he likes them he and Hunter work on the song. Garcia will play some licks and Hunter will make suggestions and they come up with the songs. It is a special relationship.

ST:    Do you have any recollections of Woodstock?

RS:    Just that it was a great time. It was revolutionary, to say the least. It represented more of a sociological phenomenon than a musical event. The reason it worked was because the community made it work. The Pranksters and the Hog Farm were there and helped pull it together. There were a lot of hassles, however. It was a logistic nightmare, for one thing. But on top of that, our gear and the gear of all the bands was loaded on to these pallets so there could be a quick transition between sets. Ours broke and we had to move all the equipment off the pallet, which resulted in a long lapse of time before we went on, with nothing happening while the equipment was being moved. Then when we went on there was supposed to be a light show behind the band. The light show screen got lowered and the wind picked it up causing this huge monstrous stage to start sliding down the hill like a sailboat leaving port because the ground was so muddy. We had to rip huge holes in it to stop the stage from sliding.

ST:    How did the concept of "An Evening with the Grateful Dead" come about, where the show would start with a New Riders set with Jerry, followed by an acoustic Dead set, and concluding with an electric Dead set?

RS:    It came about because Jerry was playing pedal steel, and digging it. John Dawson knew Jerry and asked him to play pedal steel in the New Riders. "An Evening with the Grateful Dead" worked conceptually because the music of both bands went well together. It stopped being a concept when Jerry realized that playing pedal steel was screwing with his electric guitar playing. The two instruments were so different from each that his guitar playing was suffering.

ST:    I remember seeing "An Evening with the Grateful Dead" at the Fillmore East in May 1970. There was an early show and a late show and the music would last until five in the morning. The Dead would play "That's It for the Other One" and at the end of the show the side doors of the theater would be opened and the sun would be out. It was an incredibly cosmic experience.

**RS:** The Fillmore was a magical place. I remember many mornings walking out of there and being totally amazed that the sun was out. It was like walking out of a matinee.

**ST:** Did you manage the New Riders?

**RS:** There wasn't really one manager. My involvement came during the first two albums, the first one with Jerry on it and *Powerglide*. I remember when the New Riders were living in my house. That picture on the back of the first album, where the band is leaning on the banister, was actually in my house in Kentfield. I guess you could say I was managing them at the time because pretty much all their gigs were with the Dead because Jerry was playing with them. When they got Buddy Cage they started doing shows on their own. Then Dale Franklin and Jon McIntire became their managers for a time.

**ST:** One of the concerts that is legendary was at the Fillmore West in 1970 when Miles Davis was on the same bill with the Dead.

**RS:** A lot of what we were trying to do at that time was give Graham good ideas for booking, and also play with musicians we wanted to hear. So we played with Miles Davis and Otis Redding too. That was the purpose of it all, to play with people that we wanted to hear. We worked so hard we never got a chance to hear anything.

**ST:** Were you at the Capitol Theatre show in Portchester in 1971 when the band did that ESP show?

**RS:** That was a trip that Mickey was on and he got the band interested. Dr. Stanley Krippner, a parapsychologist, was involved. The purpose was to try to get the audience to send a message to a psychic recipient who was at a different location by having the audience concentrate on some slides that were projected on a screen behind the band. As I recall the experiment was a success.

**ST:** What was the story behind the show at the Chateau d'Herouville in France in 1971?

**RS:** That was Jon McIntire's baby. Somebody just flew the band over there to play a concert but it ended up getting rained out so the band played at his house.

**ST:** Did you go to Europe with the band in 1972?

**RS:** It was an incredible experience. We carried with us a lot of recording equipment because we recorded that European tour for the live album *Europe '72*. We even carried a 16-track machine with us. I had an awful lot of responsibility because we also brought the New Riders to Europe for some gigs and I had to fly back and get them. And of course, we took everybody — all the family, all the wives, everybody. We traveled in two big buses across the continent.

**ST:** Wasn't that the Bolos and the Bozos trip?

**RS:** Yes, again that was just fun and games.

**ST:** As the Dead's popularity started growing, the band started playing larger venues. The band developed the wall of sound, which had the clearest, sweetest sound you ever wanted to hear. How did that come together?

**RS:** The wall developed slowly but surely, and then developed down scale. But as a road manager it was a nightmare. It was horribly expensive. We had four tractor trailers and our own stage to accommodate it. In fact we had two stages. While one stage was being put up, the other stage was being taken down. As a tour progressed the stages would leapfrog from one venue to the next so that it would be ready when the equipment arrived. The sound system went up almost thirty feet in the air and we had to develop the technology to get the speakers in place. We had over twenty guys to help set it up and break it down. When we would get home from this monster road tour we would have hardly any money left. We would play a tour of sold-out shows at places like the Boston Garden and break even. It wasn't cost effective and it required too much work to set up and break down.

However, that system is the reason that stereo sound systems in halls developed. The research and development that the Grateful Dead sound technicians did with the wall of sound is what developed into the fine stereo systems of today. It cost a fortune and the Grateful Dead were the only ones doing it. With the advent of digital technology and computers it became possible to have the same quality on a smaller scale. During the band's year off in 1975 we developed a much smaller compact system that had state-of-the-art sound.

**ST:** What is it about the Grateful Dead that makes them survive?

**RS:** I think that probably it comes down to the fact that they enjoy playing together and plus what they come up with is always a surprise to them as much as to us. They take risks, and they have always been on the edge of being outlaws. They are adventurous and are willing to take risks socially, chemically, musically, and do things that are unexpected. They would make records that weren't commercial, and play all night to where you'd walk outside after the show and the sun would be up. Going to a Dead show is an experience because you never know where it is going to go; it's unpredictable. The music is completely inexplicable and impossible to categorize. The Grateful Dead are mavericks and that is something that is very popular in American culture and tradition: a band willing to risk it and stand on its own two feet and be proud of what they are doing. The music continued because the band and the audience enjoy the risks they are taking musically. Pushing it to the limit, and going beyond it, and wondering where it is going to go. It's the thing of playing different songs every night and playing songs for the first time in front of an audience like a Beatles song or a Warren Zevon song. Those things aren't rehearsed, they're done on the spur-of-the-moment. No band does that. They are musically adventurous, and that is a lot of the magic about the Grateful Dead.

RICK BRACKETT

SHARYN NAKAO

JAY BLAKESBERG

JIM MARSHALL

## JERRY GARCIA, DAN HEALY,

## PHIL LESH & RAMROD

The following interview began as a rap with Grateful Dead soundman Dan Healy but ended up becoming a group discussion when band members Jerry Garcia and Phil Lesh joined in. Road crew member Larry "Ramrod" Shurtliff also had a few words to say.

ST: Dan, first I'd like to ask how many years you've been involved in sound engineering.

DH: I've got about fifteen years in professionally, where I've been doing it pretty regularly. I started out in high school playing music. I played piano and guitar in bands and stuff like that. Along about 1963 I moved into San Francisco and got a job in a little recording studio called Commercial Records. It's defunct now. At the time it was the state-of-the-art studio in San Francisco. It had a three-track tape recorder on half-inch tape. That was big time in those days, when four tracks were really rare. Eight tracks hadn't even been born yet, let alone sixteen and twenty. I worked days in this studio, and I went to school with some of the members of some of the bands and got to know them.

ST: Who was that?

DH: You're familiar with the Quicksilver Messenger Service? John Cippolina and I have known each other ever since we were kids. I used to go hang out at their practices because they would practice right next door to where I lived, in Larkspur. We lived on houseboats. I lived on one houseboat; the Quicksilver Messenger Service lived on the next houseboat over in the Corte Madera Slough in Larkspur.

You couldn't avoid hearing them play. They would be going on all day and night. I got to know these guys. Since I worked in recording studios I knew about sound so I went to a gig with them once, the third or fourth gig ever put on in the old Fillmore.

ST: What year was this?

DH: 1966. I remember going to the gig and being really prepared, because I had been hanging out with these people and had a reasonable idea of what their music was going to be like.

The sound system at the gig was just hopelessly inadequate. You couldn't hear anything. It was nothing like being at the practice. There were two small speakers on either side of the stage. The band would start playing, and as soon as they did you might as well turn off the P.A. because you couldn't hear the words or any of that kind of stuff. I remember being appalled, because I was working in recording studios, and of course was into good sound and good speakers.

I decided that I would do some sound systems for the Quicksilver Messenger Service. They had hinted to me about this, because after the gig I mentioned that I was really blown out at how bad the sound system was. So, they said, "Wow, what can we do about it?" We went and rented from this sound company in San Francisco just about all the sound equipment they had. We took the equipment to a gig one night, and stacked it up all over the place. Quicksilver and the Dead were playing that night. I'd say it was the latter part of 1965 or the first part of 1966. I guess that was the first big rock P.A.

Then we got into a scene where, because I was working in a studio which only operated from daylight to dark (8:00 to 5:00), after they locked up the studio at night we'd sneak in and record. So I would take all the bands in there. That was really a good trip.

Around that time we got booted out of the houseboats. They bulldozed them and filled in all the land to build

**Ramrod, Pigpen & Dan Healy**

condominiums. So the Quicksilver Messenger Service moved out to a town called Olema, which is in West Marin County up by the coast.

The Grateful Dead were living in a place called Camp Lagunitas, which is on the road out there in West Marin County. I knew all those guys from being at the gigs and hanging out with them.

**ST:** What was the Dead's configuration at that point?
**DH:** Bill Kreutzmann, Jerry Garcia, Bob Weir, Phil Lesh, and Pigpen—that was the Grateful Dead.

**ST:** What was Pigpen playing?
**DH:** Pigpen was playing organ. He played a Farfisa or Vox, whatever those things are called, those squeak-squeak organs.

**ST:** What type of music were the Dead playing?

**DH:** Country rock and roll. Jerry and all of the boys had a lot of bluegrass and country music background. A lot of the songs were old country tunes which were rockified. One was "Beat It On Down The Line." Weir did some old bluegrass tunes rockified, like "New Minglewood Blues," which was an old traditional bottleneck blues song updated to rock and roll.

At that time, you have to remember, there weren't very many long-haired people around and so you sort of knew everybody. There were enough of them to fill the old Fillmore, which held 400-500 people, though we would jam a thousand in there.

**ST:** Who was running the Fillmore? Bill Graham?

**DH:** No. This was before Graham. At that time Graham was involved with the San Francisco Mime Troupe. What happened was that the Fillmore Corporation used to rent the building to anyone who wanted to rent it. All you had to do was pay them $200 and you got to use the place for a night.

What we would do was get up $200 and we'd rent the place from the Fillmore Corporation and put on the gig. We would make our own posters. That's where all the posters came from, because in those days nobody had any money for radio advertising. It was a real shoestring, low-budget operation. The entire show production would be $350.

There were just about enough people that were aware of that music and that scene to fill the place. It was a tight scene. The same people came every weekend. We would rent the place and charge a buck to two bucks at the door until we'd get back the two or three hundred dollars we'd invested in the show and then let everybody else in for free.

**ST:** At this point were you with Quicksilver?

**DH:** I was never really with them. I was actually independent, working in the studio and making tapes. I wasn't deeply involved in doing P.A. systems, I was just in an advisory capacity. My career was in the recording studio. It was happening and I was having a good time doing that. But I was interested and concerned that these guys have good sound systems and be heard, because it was cool music. The instant I heard it, it was like I'd heard it somewhere before. I inherently identified with it. I didn't even have to think about it. It outraged me that they were being burnt off by horrible sound systems. We would get together the sound equip-

It was pretty loose. It was really a good scene. There was very little money; the whole vibe of sharing was what was happening in those days. It was one of those situations where nobody ever really had anything, but nobody ever really needed anything. It was kind of magic that way. We had what we were doing and that was basically all we needed. Everyone had a place to sleep, and clothes to wear, and food to eat.

One of my best memories, biggest get-offs, and best buzzes is how we used to party and blow out. We'd start partying some Friday and get really stoned and hang out. Come Sunday morning we'd all decide to go play live in Golden Gate Park. We'd play in the Panhandle. This was around 1967. So we would decide on Sunday morning. At about 8 or 9 o'clock somebody would run out and rent a flatbed truck and a small generator. We used to pull the truck up in front of 710, throw all the equipment on it and roar over to the park. We'd start up our generator and start playing. We had it down.

From about '67 on I hung out with the Dead only. That's when I really began getting just into that trip.

In those days we were also making an album, *Anthem of the Sun*, the second album; the first album was *The Golden Road*, which was produced by Dave Hassinger, who was a staff production engineer for Warner Brothers Records at the time. So the band did the first album with them. Apparently the band didn't get off too much behind it, nor did Warner Brothers or Hassinger.

It was cut in three or four days. In those days you went in and had all your material together. You just laid down all the songs and the producer would mix them down and put them on the tape. That was done on a four track. In fact, when we were mixing down the movie to get some flash-back excerpts, we got the old masters to that album. Old four-track tapes; it was really interesting.

**ST:** Were there any out-takes from that album?

**DH:** I don't think so. That particular record was the first and only one that was exclusively prepared by the record company side of the operation, by a staff producer. So, we never saw any out-takes. There weren't lots of out-takes on anything. You would use three rolls of tape in making an album. There wouldn't have been forty rolls of out-takes like there is these days.

135

**ST:** Wasn't the whole concept of improvisational music in rock and roll, like "Viola Lee Blues," unique then?

**DH:** That was another thing. The record company wanted all the songs to be 2½ minutes long. It was a compromise to get them on there. I think that was probably solely what got the band bugged about it.

By then I had logged quite a bit of time in recording studios — three or four years of ass-kicking, everyday studio use doing a lot of commercial jingles, and some rock and roll songs. I recorded Paul Revere and the Raiders, a couple of old hit records, and obscure local San Francisco hits.

It was time for the Dead to do another album, so they were going back into the studio. By then, eight tracks had just come out and there weren't any in San Francisco, but there were in L.A. The band decided to go to L.A. to record an album, again with Warner Brothers and Dave Hassinger. By then I was traveling with them and doing sound live at gigs, so I went to L.A. with the band.

I had outgrown the studio that I had been working in, in San Francisco. Several of the groups had asked me to take them into the studio and I was using everybody's studios because these were record company situations. I would just go rent the time and take the group in. I was using Coast, Golden State, and another small studio that was built for the Kingston Trio. That was a three-track studio, but they had just ordered an eight-track machine at about the time the Grateful Dead went to L.A. to work on *Anthem of the Sun*, and they were converting their board. It was a tiny room in the basement of an old building in North Beach in San Francisco.

Upstairs on the ground floor was a Zim's (a hamburger joint in San Francisco). There used to be a secret fire escape stairwell at the back of the studio. You could go up and come in through the bathrooms at Zim's. So you could sneak out of the studio and sneak upstairs and grab raw burgers. It was really cool. You could get food and it enabled you to be in the studio for days at a time without having to go outside. That was one of the real neat aspects of it. You could be really into doing what you were doing, and not have to tear yourself away and get into another groove.

Since I was using other studios, I had quit my job at Commercial Recorders. They were into lots of commercial work, and I wanted to get more into music production. I decided to find a place where I could record good rock and roll. So the band came down to L.A. and I came down with them.

At that time Danny Rifkin and Rock Scully were the managers of the Grateful Dead. They had booked a tour to the East Coast, which was the first time the band ever went out of California, almost literally the first time out of San Francisco. In New York we played at the Electric Circus, with all the flashing lights and mirrors.

At this point Jerry Garcia entered the room.

**DH:** Hey man ... [speaking to Garcia]

**JG:** Wow, heavy. Healy doin' an interview.

**DH:** Anyway, we went to L.A. and laid down the basic tracks for several of the songs. What we were going to do was go back East to do some work in recording studios while we were playing there. We went back to New York City and stayed at the Chelsea Hotel for a month or two. We were playing gigs at nights and on the weekends, and recording in the studio. Century Sound was one, and Olmstead was the other studio. They were eight-track studios, which was state-of-the-art in those days.

    The whole matter of having to compromise the music to fit within the production ideas of Dave Hassinger and the record industry was really hanging everybody up a lot. So, there got to be friction between the band and Hassinger — hassles back and forth. We were at a session one afternoon when we got into an argument with Hassinger about something he was doing in the mix. He jumped up, freaked out, and stomped out of the studio. Everybody just sat there. We were left there halfway through finishing the record.

    I'm talkin' about *Anthem of the Sun*. [to Garcia]

    We were left to finish off the record, so we did. That was the turning point. We had about half of it laid down in the studio, and by that time we were all really intrigued by the possibilities of what we were doing live.

**JG:** When we went to New York we had laid down the first part of "The Other One," the slow part, and a basic for "New Potato Caboose." We were working on "Born Cross-Eyed." That's as much as we had gotten done. At that point we were going about it almost straight.

**DH:** Like takes, laying down songs, and breaking it into basic tracks. When that got finished, we got into the live possibility, which looked really interesting. We decided that we could collect a bunch of live tapes. We began recording with a small one-quarter-inch four-track machine. That was big time in those days, because four track was big time, and one-quarter-inch tape meant that it was possible that we could afford to buy tape. The machine was an old Viking deck that the Bear made by taking two stereo machines and splicing them together into one machine. It was a real funky machine. You had to set it down and have a talk with it, warm it up, and if you got it just in the right mood, then it would record for you, and cease to stop and warble. We collected about ten gigs' worth of tapes.

**ST:** Where were those shows?

**JG:** The northwest tour and the Carousel Ballroom.

**DH:** The Crystal Ballroom in Portland was one of them, and the King's Beach Bowl in Lake Tahoe was another. Somehow we had a real half-inch four track for the gig, and that was like the big time.

**JG:** It was the big four track that we used for the main bit of the live "Other One."

**DH:** I just remember it was in the big black box. Those days were before mixing boards or consoles. We had all these small four-channel mixers, which would be stacked up to the ceiling, dozens of them all wired so they would filter down onto the tape tracks.

We got all these tapes, and they were all recorded on different machines in different cities. The speeds were all different and weird and variable. There would be things wrong. The performance would be going along real good and, all of a sudden, someone would kick out a plug, or the power would go off and the performance would be ended prematurely.

We got back into the studio and it turned out that there wasn't one performance that played all the way through and did anything. We decided that what we would do was just devise a way to be able to play them all by aligning and starting two different performances in the same place, and comparing the different meters and rhythms.

**JG:** Four stereo pairs of completely different shows that all started in the same meter and had about the same tuning. We keyed them all off at the "boo da da da da da da da da da bow."

**ST:** It took me a few years to notice many of the edits on that album.

**JG:** That's because there are zillions of them. They're everywhere, all over the fucking place. A lot of them are not in obvious places at all. There are things like three or four splices every two or three bars, and in a couple of transiuonal places where we would have to piece things together to get it to work.

The performances were all on different tape mediums, and there wasn't the ability to have four four tracks all in one studio so that you could make it easy on yourself, just put on all the tapes and work through them. You had to convert. Columbus Recording had three two tracks, a mono, a three track and an eight track, which was a brand-new thing that was the hot dog machine. We had to convert all the performances down to whatever tape machine there was in the studio. Some of the performances we took down to the three track; some we took down to the two track just so that we could have enough machines to simultaneously run it all. Then we transferred it all on to the eight-track machine. It took almost a year.

DH: At Columbus Recording, that studio in the basement I was telling you about.

JG: We weren't making a record in the normal sense; we were making a collage. We were trying to do something completely different, which didn't even have to do with a concept. It had to do with an approach that's more like electronic music or concrete music where you are actually assembling bits and pieces toward an enhanced non-realistic representation. That is really the sense of what we were doing.

ST: The first side of that record really creates a mood. In certain sections you really feel purple.

JG: So did we.

DH: By then we were hopelessly overdue to the record company because they had frameworks they like to see projects get done in.

ST: You really must have had to pull their arms to get this whole project going.

JG: No, we didn't, because they were foolish enough to let us execute a contract in which we had no limit as to studio time. Before that, they were used to dealing with conventional acts where nobody ever spent more than two weeks making a record.

ST: You only had two cuts on the entire album. Didn't you have any political frictions with the record company because of this?

JG: No, because we also had complete artistic control. We knew we would run into something like that before we even started, or even had a concept of recording.

**DH:** Yeah, it was heading in that direction.

**ST:** So who finally mixed that album, and edited it?

**JG:** It went on over a long period of time. Me and Healy and Phil.

**ST:** You finally got all the tapes together and said "This is it, this is *Anthem of the Sun?"*

**JG:** No, it was actually more careful. It was a structural product, 'cause it all ended up on two pieces of continuous sides of eight track tape. The way we went at it, we shot at performances of the mix rather than mixing little bits and tying them together. We ended up mixing almost the whole side in big flows to get smoothness through the transitions. It was the most complicated fucking mixing you would ever imagine. If one fader wasn't down when it was supposed to be — BAM — this big loud noise would come through. It took a long time, but we took lots and lots of passes and then went through the best of them. Maybe we edited a couple of times, but not too much really.

**DH:** Actually, the one part of it we did have together was that, even though we didn't have a defined final picture, we built it in such a fashion as we were putting it together that it was pretty much obvious how it was going to be mixed. That's where a lot of the time went in, actually constructing the master eight-track tape from all the live and studio combinations.

**JG:** Healy was great. Man, there would be times when he would be there with a thumb on the capstan motor of two machines, slowing down the speed.

**DH:** This was way before the days of variable speed.

**JG:** It was part of the thing of having two different recordings of one performance and trying to get them to be in phase.

**DH:** Some of them were recorded at 7½, and some were recorded at 3¾.

**JG:** It was really a fucking ordeal from a technical standpoint, because we anticipated all the shit that later would have really made it all the easier. We had to gimmick it. Almost no studios at the time even had pan pots. We had to do two channel panning with faders which is, in a way, more sensitive. A lot of things of that sort we had to really invent to make work.

**DH:** Not having pan pots is one of the reasons why it doesn't have an identifiable sound like most records do. Everything nowadays is pan pots, so all panning in motion on records has a certain texture that you can inherently identify. When you do your own pan out of two faders that never really move across symetrically, it has a more human influence.

All of the things were that way. All of the speed corrections and inaccuracies, the splices and the mixes were based on jury-rigging it out of some piece of gear that wasn't really designed to do that. As a result, nothing was really stock sounding. Everything had its own way of motion and movement and character to it, which, in a way, was one of the great things that state-of-the-art modern-day studios have left behind.

JG:  They have softened that organic possibility of having something that sounds like nothing you've ever heard before.

DH:  It's harder and harder to do that.

ST:  Did you actually ever play one continuous jam that's representative of the first side of *Anthem*?

JG:  Yeah, sure. That was partly what it was a model of, but never as concisely or with as infinite detail. It was mostly the detail we were after, the thing of incredible detail.

ST:  When you remixed that album, it really brought Bobby's rhythm out a lot more.

JG:  Phil and Dan did that.

ST:  That was great. It added new dynamics.

DH:  I listen to them both now. They're both really groovy in their own ways. I think it was merely a different version of it.

JG:  It's one of an almost infinite number of possibilities. It's the performance thing. Each performance of the mix of those eight tracks is like throwing the I Ching. You know it will all work. Any possibility will work; any combination would produce a version of it that you could dig.

ST:  Are you guys happy with that album?

DH:  I think at the time we were.

JG:  Sure. We mixed it for the hallucinations and it worked great.

ST:  I feel that album was a breakthrough for the whole rock scene.

JG:  Nobody else thought so except us, although some parts of it sound remarkably far out even now. It's amazing that it hasn't dated very much. There are places of extreme awkwardness, but it wasn't hurting for imagination.

ST:  How come you decided not to do the introduction or

ending to "The Other One" anymore?

**JG:** It wasn't happening for me emotionally. Certain songs stop being viable because they are not graceful enough to keep performing in a natural way. In other words, we could play those tunes, but we would have to rehearse the fuck out of them, and part of our whole trip is staying interested. There was a time when we performed all that material really regularly and we used it up.

**DH:** We also had a lot of fun playing with the versions of the record. It was a crack-up to pull off things that were changes due to mechanical differences in the studio. Seeing if you could perform them live was a lot of fun. There were a lot of quirks in it they learned to play.

**ST:** The next album after that was *Aoxomoxoa*. Did you mix that?

**DH:** That one was a real group effort.

**JG:** It started off down at Pacific Recording with Bob and Betty, in a real offhand way. It ended up with everyone involved in it. Remember "Barbed Wire Whipping Party?" We had some great out-takes from that record.

**DH:** That was probably the beginning of famous out-takes around an album. By then we had enough of a recording budget, and the state-of-the-art of the studios had advanced enough that there were things like stashes of tape that you could pull in the studio.

**JG:** Sixteen tracks too.

**DH:** The very first Ampex 16 track was in this studio. Ampex was right in that neighborhood in San Mateo. This is where we first met Ron Wickersham, who is now Rick Turner's partner in Alembic. He was on the staff that designed the first Ampex color video machine, which became the model for the 16-track tape recorder. He also had a moonlight gig at this studio. He had come to one of our gigs, and was impressed by our sound, our equipment, and our music. We began hanging out with him, and he took us to the studio and turned us on to the 16 track. So we began recording *Aoxomoxoa* down there. It was the turning point of record overdubs.

**JG:** It was also the beginning of really serious collaboration between Bob Hunter and myself. We began to write a lot of tunes together.

**ST:** *Aoxomoxoa* has a very distinctive sound, more so than some of the other ones.

**DH:** It came out pretty good.

**JG:** The tunes are what I liked about it. The performances were a little bit twisted.

**RR:** "What's Become of the Baby."

**JG:** Yeah, Garcia's madcap excursions into utter weirdness.

**ST:** The next album after that was *Live Dead*.

**JG:** Right. *Live Dead* is actually contemporary with it and, in fact, we finished the mix of it before we finished *Aoxomoxoa*.

**ST:** Where was *Live Dead* recorded?

**JG:** At the Carousel[2] and the Avalon. We did two nights each, I think. They were the first 16-track location recordings.

**ST:** What year was that?

**JG:** Early '69.

**ST:** Are the tunes on the first three sides, specifically "Dark Star," "Saint Stephen," "The Eleven," and "Turn On Your Lovelight," all part of one jam, or were they assembled from different shows?

**JG:** I think they may be from two different nights, but they are fundamentally one performance. Actually, the out-takes of the album I've heard recently are, in my opinion, better performances of the same material. At that time, we constructed the whole thing as a show. It was all a complete long piece.

**ST:** Do you think you'll ever do "The Eleven" again?

**JG:** It's possible, man. Anything is possible. There's no way I could say we would never do it.

**ST:** At that time the idea of having one jam on three sides of a double album was innovative in rock music.

**JG:** It was really only innovative if you look at it in terms of rock and roll or pop. Jazz players like Coltrane have been doing that for years.

**ST:** What was the personnel of the band, sound crew, and road crew at that time?

**DH:** The band was Jerry, Phil, Bob, Bill, Mickey, Pig, and TC. TC was there for a while, but he went on to study music. The road crew and sound crew were all the same people in those days. It wasn't organized like it is now. The people involved in the crew were Ramrod, Hagen, Jackson, Matthews, and myself.

**ST:** What about Betty?

**JG:** Betty wasn't on the road with us. She started working the

[2]The majority of *Live Dead* was recorded at the Fillmore West, which had previously been the Carousel.

Carousel, then she started working second for Matthews. Then down at San Mateo, she got her first licks on *Aoxomoxoa* and subsequent live stuff.

DH: She did live recordings at the Carousel. The Bear was with us then, working on the P.A. and other things. He had devised a couple of new ideas. He was working with Buklah, making some synthesizer equipment, and he also had developed a new speaker system. The "bananas," he called them. They were actually the forerunner of our P.A. today. It consisted of a cabinet with a bunch of 15-inch JBL speakers in it, but each one of them was 12 feet tall. To use them properly you'd have to stand them one on top of another, which of course was impossible, because the Carousel, which is where we were first using them, had about a 15-foot ceiling. But we used them. It was an uncanny, weird P.A. system, and seemed to work pretty good. The next big development in sound systems beyond that was probably the Altamont show. That was where the final model of the bananas really got set up, because it was outside with an unlimited amount of room for all this stuff.

ST: Didn't Bear front you guys a whole sound system?
JG: He didn't actually front it. We traded it back to him for freedom. That was as early as 1966, before we even got a record contract together. After that we had gone through a great element of doubt as to his ability to officially deliver the goodies. So we did a whole variety of things. We got into a more reactionary approach to it, thinking that what we wanted to do was just be able to fucking play and not have to hassle with all that shit.

ST: What type of equipment were you using in those days, Fender amps?
JG: Yeah. I'm using the same black-faced twin reverb now, as a pre-amp.
RR: The good shit lasts.

ST: What were the dimensions of the Carousel?
DH: It held about eight hundred people, not very many at all, though we would put as many in there as we could get. It was an old ballroom left over from the Swing era. It was owned by an Irishman.
JG: They had Irish music there on Thursday nights.
DH: That's all they had in there. Aside from that it was closed all the time, and had been closed down right after the Swing

era. It was still in its original state, right out of the '20s, right down to the chandeliers in the place. The interior was beautiful. It wasn't at all torn up; it was in mint condition.

Matthews and I met this guy who happened to have a four-track tape machine we wanted to rent, at a place called Emerald Studios. He was in the Irish League in San Francisco and knew about this place. We were looking around for places to play. He said, "Hey, I know where there is this ballroom," so he took Matthews and me over there. Here was this beautiful old ballroom.

So, we went back and talked to Rock Scully and Danny Rifkin. We decided to cook up a plan to see if we could score it and do some gigs there. We got hold of the people and they were real good about it. They said, "Sure, you want the place, take it." So we built our own stage in there and put on our own rock and roll shows.

**ST:** What kind of sound system were you pushing?
**DH:** In those days we had an Altec P.A. There was a period where we just had a store-bought P.A. although it was modified, but we bought Altec equipment. That was sort of the introduction of large bass cabinets and big, long throw horns. We used that all through the Carousel days up until when Alembic was formed.

At that time we had moved out to Marin County. We had a practice hall up in northern Marin, near Hamilton Air Force Base. In this hall we had our practice complex set up, and there was this old shed out back. That became the technical electronics shop, where we would work on stuff. Owsley, Wickersham, Rick Turner, Matthews, and Betty and all of us would go out there to try building our own pickups, guitars, and amplifiers. Garcia would come in there and tear his guitar apart in the afternoon. That was a great place.

**JG:** That was fun. We got a lot of shit done there. That's where we smashed the shit out of Weir's Acoustic amplifier. We executed it, jumped up and down on it.

**DH:** Weir had this horrible Acoustic amplifier that had a horn like the ones under the hood of cop cars. It was a big cabinet, and it had this horn right at the top, right at ear level. It was just murder, pain every time he'd play it. Your ears would fall right out of your sockets. So finally we couldn't stand it any more. One day we decided to sacrifice the amplifier, and we destroyed it right on the spot. That was great. We were seeing appendages of that nailed to the wall for months. That was where the Alembic thing got formed, about 1970/71.

ST: Those years must have represented some sort of turning point for you. For one thing, Graham closed down the Fillmores.

JG: Actually, quite a lot was crowded into about a 2½ or 3-year period from about late '68 to '72.

DH: A lot of changes on a lot of levels. The music was changing, the places we were playing were changing.

JG: TC left the band. We were picking up the pieces from managerial disasters. A lot of changes went down.

ST: I have fond memories of the Fillmore East. It had really good sound.

JG: That's one of the advantages when you have a permanent place; you've got it knocked for sound. You can really tune the sucker 'cause you're dealing with things that aren't changing on you every five minutes.

ST: In San Francisco you almost always play at Winterland.

JG: Yeah, but it has a problem that I spotted the last time we played there. The house is a little small for a big room, and large for a small room, so it always takes a night or so to adjust to it. It's a little bit freakish. You don't play in rooms like that often enough to get used to it. In a way, that's how you'd most like it to be, because when it's tuned right and everybody's used to it, the sense is that everything's coming from everywhere. That's the only room I can remember that behaves like that.

In a big room you hear yourself clearly on stage, and then there's another large sound beyond which is Healy in the house. That's a certain kind of groove which is easy to unfold. It's one reason you can play big rooms and they're not too freakish.

In the theaters there's an articulate kind of groove. The loudest elements seem to be coming from the stage. The blend of the vocals and all that is real pretty.

Winterland is in a completely different category. It's the only place that has that square, more height than depth feel.

DH: There's a heavy arch in the ends of the room which reflects sound.

ST: What was the problem with the '74 sound system?

JG: It was exceptional in some ways, and in some ways it was fucked. It was very good for instrumental clarity, but it wasn't too good for the drums or vocals.

Winterland Arena, San Francisco

**ST:**   It wasn't too good for the roadies either, I imagine.

**JG:**   Well, it wasn't too good economically either. It was a hell of a scene.

**ST:**   Didn't you control your dynamics more from the stage at that point?

**JG:**   Everything was controlled from the stage, but the point is that we still lacked the perspective that Healy provides in performances. That's the perspective of one guy out there who's deciding what to do with the mix, and who has enough experience to know what's meant by the music. He makes the room sound the way he thinks we meant it to. His taste and judgment is right up the alley; as right on as anybody can get.

**DH:**   The function I perform is to do two things. One is that I interface the sound system to the room mechanically. Every room has echoes and reverberances at different frequencies. I tune the room so that all the notes are audible and clear and sound good. Before the show starts you've already set the levels of the instruments. After it starts you do a musical tuning to the room. Beyond that, the other facet of what I do is to bring everybody into the system, so that there's a workable level of dynamics when they're playing.

The P.A. is stereo, and the placement is generally like people are standing on the stage, so that if you heard it without the P.A. it would just sound like a quieter version of the same thing. Generally for the first couple of songs I put very little but the vocal in the P.A. and I listen to the band. I see how each person starts adjusting their tonality, because these guys are doing the same thing. For the first couple of songs they concentrate mostly on what kind of report they're hearing back from the room from their instruments; what notes sound good and which don't. So we acquiesce to tuning through the first couple of songs. Then what theoretically happens is that you reach a place where it's in tune and the whole consideration of tuning on that level falls away. Then it's more into the musical aspects.

**ST:**   There are points in the show where the music builds to a crescendo, and the sound pressure level seems to increase. Is that done on the stage, or do you do it?

**DH:**   That's done on the stage, but not in an intentional manner. When everybody gets loose and warmed up and in the groove, and the room gets tuned in, the music seems to get louder. It's working as one force together, rather than individual forces all working at the same time. Often the sound pressure level meter goes up, but the meters that register the power being used by the P.A. will go down.

ST: When you transfer to a record, how are the dynamics of the music going to be limited by the inherent qualities of the medium?

DH: If you get the realism believable, good sounding, and rich enough, you won't have to worry about the quality of the vinyl or tape hiss.

JG: Norrnally in a live performance, when you have dynamics they are compressed. One of our big problems in recording live is that our dynamics exceed tape noise on the bottom and saturation at the top. You either get real hissy quiet music or real fucking pushed loud music.

 The whole idea is to try to communicate music to the mind, rather than to a medium as such. That goes for the live performing situation too. The whole idea is to be able to more clearly describe phase and time. Those elements that tell you about what's happening to the music in your head are much more significant information than volume.

ST: *Live Dead* seemed to convey more realistically the live concert experience than *Steal Your Face*. That one was disjointed rather than a total concept, where *Live Dead* took you right there.

JG: *Live Dead* was basically from one performance. That gives it the advantage of consistency. We're looking at a way of fine tuning that idea.

ST: There seems to be some emotional peaks, especially in the longer pieces of music, that capture the essence of the Grateful Dead.

JG: That's for you to say; I can't tell you what it is. We only know it subjectively, and I've already had my version of it cancelled enough times to know by sums and differences that my version of what the Grateful Dead sounds like is not entirely accurate. Dan Healy knows what the Grateful Dead sound like more than any one other person. We're all involved with the music, so we have to be continually checking with each other to see where it's at.

ST: The basic structure of one of your shows is a first set with a number of individual songs, and maybe a jam or a longer song at the end of the set. Then in the second set you get more into improvisational music. That's the Dead's trademark. That's what people go to see, when you really hang loose.

JG: The sense to it is that in the first set we're adjusting and fine tuning as we go; we don't want to be locked into one vehicle. You don't want to commit yourself to a long idea because something might be fucked. Suppose the sound is fucked, or your instrument breaks, or everything goes out of adjustment, and you're stuck there?

The thing is that everything has to settle down, from the strings on the guitars to the drum heads. All the grooves have to be tuned. So, the more possibilities we can throw out in the first set, the more we can tune, and feel out the personality of the individual night in terms of the audience, the room, what we are like that night, and how we are agreeing. We can find out what's possible and what isn't. It's all intuitive; we never say that we have established a certain trend. Each time it is all new. We're still trying to focus higher and higher; it gets to be a more complex possibility as we go along.

DH: There's nothing you can necessarily hold on to, and have apply the next day. The mix at the end of every show results in the knobs winding up in a certain place, and you feel you got through that barrier. You would immediately assume that you could hang on to it, but when you come in the next night, not one setting will apply in any way at all. I've gone to the extent of not letting anyone move a microphone on the stage and telling people to do just what they did the night before, just to see how pursuable something like that is. The further you pursue it, the more you realize it cannot be done.

JG: Electrons are like magic, and a fundamental part of what makes the universe seem to be a physical event. They don't make decisions based on predictability, so everything changes, including capacitances.

An electric guitar is an electromagnetic phenomenon which is really a model of what we are. It's an amplifier in a weird way; all the voltage is generated by moving the metal strings.

The capacitance of a player changes from night to night as the individual neural networks of a human being change. You're dealing with mediums where tiny increments of electron flows are significant. I'm moving a string that's a hundredth of an inch in diameter, and I have to be able to control it. The whole thing is that delicately balanced. Any slight change in humidity or temperature affects us; three new fat people in the audience and the whole fucking room is different. No room is totally predictable because the audience contour changes. You're dealing with a completely changeable interior topography.

ST: With regard to your longer pieces of music, do you plan out the jams, or are they more spontaneous?

JG: We sometimes have a loose idea of a sequence, but there's a degree of free association involved. It's not all conscious, but nobody is working blind either. Everybody deals with what they are hearing; I'm hearing a complicated network of harmony coming from the keyboards, and hearing Weir playing incredible extensions. Keys and melodic references are continually shifting.

ST: You seem to go through phases where you are either more structured or heavily into improvisation. What accounts for this?

DH: There's a cycle. Some periods are more conducive to jamming or enlarging portions of the songs. Some tours will be real deep in stretching out between songs, others will be more in the songs' groove. The songs feel good at the time. Other nights, no matter how well you're doing that, it's not what's happening. What's happening is taking songs apart, going inside them and seeing what else is in there.

JG: If we were able to tell you what it is, we wouldn't have to bother doing it. One of the most important things about this whole exercise for us is whether it will stay interesting and fun. We've been able to stay interested in spite of how bent we get. That indefinability is part of the fundamentally mysterious quality of the thing. We can't say what it is, but everybody who goes to a Grateful Dead concert knows.

ST: I think you captured that experience of a Dead concert in the movie.

DH: That was a moment of time, but in an overall view any slice of time is representative of every slice of time. There is no one version of the experience, nor a single definition.

JG: No one viewpoint is the one. I'm attracted to my own version of it, just like you're attracted to yours, but I also know other versions of it are equally happening.

ST: What do you see happening with your sound system in the future?

DH: Smaller and higher quality sound is the thing. I want to get the system small enough without sacrificing quality so that I can bring more sound equipment out for other parts of the room, to expand the scope of what you hear into a truly spherical three-dimensional situation. That offers the audience more information, and more trips to get off on. At Winterland I put separate sound systems up and downstairs, and fed different information into them.

Any sound should have the quality of being moveable, of appearing from anywhere. This would take realism off the stage, move it out into the room. I'm into the guys in the back of the room. You should have a better handle on how to recreate what you're not close enough to the stage to know is happening.

JG: It's easy to sit in the primo seats and hear good. The guy in the movie who knows all the words to the tunes and sings along, conducts the band. He should be able to go to the back of the room, take the last seat in the house, and conduct the whole room.

ST: So you're thinking of using a quad system like Pink Floyd's?

DH: Quad is a concept of four speakers in four corners. It could be a limitation for the type of music we play.

JG: Pink Floyd's music is constructed very simply so that they can take a piece of the music and spin it. Maybe the guy who's playing it can tell what's happening, but I doubt it. In that sense they have music that is more highly organized than ours, and not nearly so complex at any given instant. So making decisions about spinning it is easier.

I personally am not interested in sacrificing control over my instrument for the gimmick of having it come from far away from me just for the effect. I don't want to create an objective experience for everybody in the room. I'm more interested in what the mind does. I want it to be subjective for each person, just like it is for me.

DH: There are subtle levels of motion that can come out psychoacoustically. That's what I meant when I said I'd like to bring some more equipment to put in the room and not on the stage. You could technically say we will have a quad system, but this is more of an environmental situation and less of a gimmick. You'll hear the sound come from four different points of view, and not hear one thing move to four different places. It's more subtle. You might not even pick up on it, but I do enough different things that everyone at least picks up some of it.

It's like the subtleties that go into our albums; we go

through hours of meticulous work mixing things. On a lot of our records, you'll hear a whole different album if you listen on earphones. There are cases of instruments playing whole other melodies that you can only hear that way. If you get those albums, there's always another layer of stuff you can get into, in addition to what immediately jumps out at you.

The live P.A. is just an extension of this concept, whereby you experience what you want based on whatever you think you heard. Never knowing for sure what I heard and never being able to predict it is one of the things that keeps me interested. That unpredictability is what keeps things interesting for our audiences too. As soon as you're sure what's going on, it's not a big deal anymore, and it's no longer fun. The whole name of the game clear down to the bottom line is fun.

Through use of the P.A. I have discovered ways to keep people interested and keep it fun for everyone. That's why I do it.

ST: Electronic equipment is sensitive. Doesn't the constant moving and loading tend to cause breakdowns when you're on the road?

DH: The power amps are the main problem because they are the heavies for the size. Often at the end of a tour they're laying in rubble at the bottom of the boxes. The smaller electronic equipment tends to hold up better. If anything does break down, we have enough people in the road crew so that collectively we have the know-how to fix just about anything.

PL: I'm a Mac man myself. I remember the time we sent one of our guys to the MacIntosh factory in Binghamton, New York, when we were doing the Watkins Glen gig. We flew him in with $8,000 and dropped him in the parking lot by helicopter on a Saturday. The man from the Grateful Dead comes from out of the sky. Half of the employees came in on their day off to put together the amps that were near completion on the assembly line.

ST: How do you contemplate a gig like Watkins Glen?

PL: We put a tremendous amount of planning into that gig. We practically had to do it ourselves, despite the promoters. The biggest hassle was convincing the Band to come out and play. Hey, man, it's just down the road a piece. Come on out and play. What can you lose? They played great!

HERB GREENE

## TOM CONSTANTEN

TC was a member of the Grateful Dead for little more than a year but during his tenure with the band his influence was significant. Whether by design or by fate he was a member of the band during the height of its improvisational and experimental period. TC is a classically trained keyboardist who met Phil Lesh at UC Berkeley in 1961 and became close friends with him because of their shared love of music.

**ST:** How did you get involved with the Grateful Dead?

**TC:** I met Phil Lesh at UC Berkeley in the early '60s when he was 21 and I was 17. We shared musical interests and an apartment in Berkeley. Phil had been at the College of San Mateo playing trumpet in the jazz band, had written some jazz charts for them, and had also discovered some of the Stockhausen pieces I was into. We took a class together with Luciano Berio at Mills College in Oakland.

Phil also had been hanging out with Jerry Garcia. Jerry was staying in Palo Alto at the time before there was the Grateful Dead. Jerry played regularly at a place called the Tangent on University Avenue in Palo Alto.

In 1962 I went to study in Europe. Berio set up scholarships so I could study with him, Boulez, Stockhausen, and Pousseur in Europe, which lasted more than a year. When I got back to the States in 1964 I moved to the Bay Area. This was when the rock and roll universe started to expand. Sometime in 1965 Phil was asked to join the Grateful Dead, which at that time was called the Warlocks. Eventually I got the invitation to join the fun.

**ST:** When did you join the band?

**TC:** November 1968.

**ST:** I understand that before you were formally a member of the band you recorded some tracks for the *Anthem of the Sun* album.

**TC:** I was unable to avoid the draft so I got stuck in the Air Force for a couple of years. But I was able to sneak away on occasion and I contributed to the *Anthem of the Sun* recording sessions as well as the *Aoxomoxoa* recording sessions. On *Anthem*, I played prepared piano, did some electronic things, and the opening piano part of "Alligator." On *Aoxomoxoa* I provided keyboard arrangements on all of the songs except "Rosemary."

**ST:** What exactly is "prepared piano?"

**TC:** You put things like screws, coins, or clothes pins inside the piano strings to make them sound different. I did one effect where I took a dime-store gyroscope, gave it a good spin, and put that up against the sounding board of the piano. It sounded like a chain saw being taken to the piano. Producer Dave Hassinger cleared his seat by a foot and a half when he heard it being done.

**ST:** The *Anthem of the Sun* album essentially consisted of two long pieces of music — "That's It for the Other One" into

"New Potato Caboose" into "Born Cross-Eyed" on Side 1 and "Alligator" into "Caution" on Side 2. This style of playing was not common for rock music at that time.

TC: That was one of the things that attracted me to the band. The *Anthem* album is sort of a bizarre document, a studio attempt to recreate what the band was doing in concert where one tune would segue into another. "Alligator" into "Caution" was a sequence we could embark on and go sailing for 45 minutes at least. The first live album is also an example of that. The sequence of "Dark Star" into "St. Stephen" into "The Eleven" into "Lovelight," although by that time it was getting modular. There were choices at any given point and many of the choices were even made *ad hoc*, on the stage at the time they were being made. It was occasionally amusing to see when Weir would be taking the band into one tune and Jerry would be taking the band into another. You would have these tidal frictions of a thought or direction where the band wanted to go and that was developing at that time. It was an exciting time for that reason.

ST: Your keyboard playing seemed to hold the band together when the band was improvising and, yet at the same time, cause the jams to expand.

TC: The Grateful Dead were able to rehearse it well enough so that they had a high percentage of things they discovered that worked. Although as anyone who had listened to the band time after time after time would know, some performances are better than others. That's a chance you have to take in courting serendipity — sometimes serendipity comes to grace your performances and sometimes not. As far as some of the farther out improvisations and directions, there were already tendencies in that direction among the band members, of which I was happy to be congruently in step with, although it might be an over-estimate to say I was a driving force in that direction. Conversely, I think I might have had an influence on some of the more simple harmonic tunes the band got into shortly after I left, as in *Workingman's Dead* and *American Beauty*. So there were two tidal directions going at the same time.

ST: I understand that the band practiced quite a bit for songs like "The Eleven."

TC: The band practiced all sorts of odd time signatures. There was also a ten Mickey brought in and a fifteen that we tried — anything to break out of that square mold of threes or fours. Also, having more than one drummer, it gave them something to do that was more interesting.

**ST:** Some of the "Dark Star"s the band played in 1969 were quite long and varied.

**TC:** They were exploratory ventures — possibly you could use the word "experimental" for that — it's not so much a set piece that you know where you are in it and know where you're gonna go, as you're out on an ocean in a boat and you can choose your landmarks and response to things and move in certain directions as you wish — of course, always interacting.

**ST:** The band responds well to each other's nuances.

The Septet at Golden Hall, San Diego Community Concourse, January 10, 1970

**TC:** If you are going to be that free, you have to. It's a deliberate choice. Jerry has always been that way — it's part of his makeup — it's part of his nature. The music requires it and the situation encouraged it.

It's the opposite of what I call, disparagingly, the Android Jukebox Syndrome, which you can do wearing a tie and a happy face and you need not be mentally present — which is exactly what we weren't interested in.

**ST:** It seemed like the "Dark Star"'s were more experimental, going out farther, when you were in the band.

**TC:** The thing that I liked about it is the proportion of how much that song in particular gives you in terms of places to explore relative to the effort it takes to maintain. It is especially favorable to the performer.

**ST:** At that time it seemed that the band had developed certain melodic themes which were occasionally interwoven into the middle of jams. For instance during "Dark Star," the band would play the theme that became "Uncle John's Band" in the middle of the song.

**TC:** We would play a long extended improvisationary piece that went a lot of places. You find jazz players doing that. Sometimes it works and sometimes it doesn't. That's part of the chemical thing. But if you're there, you should try. One of the ten figures we played became "Playing in the Band," though no one knew it at the time. Anything could happen, not to mention segues. The "Dark Star" into "St. Stephen" into "The Eleven" into "Lovelight" pattern wasn't cast in cement. There were occasional "Dark Star"'s into "The Other One" segues and "The Other One" into "New Potato Caboose" was another of these long trains, so to speak.

**ST:** "New Potato Caboose" got dropped from the repertoire.

**TC:** If you listen to it on record, it was kind of produced with harpsichord and organ in a way that could only happen in the studio. There's one organ segment where Pigpen and I sat side by side to play it because there were so many notes. As it turned out, it was too impractical to perform live so we had to go for the same effect on the recording.

**ST:** Would you agree that the Dead's music has a certain amount of inspiration from what jazz artists were doing in the late fifties and '60s?

**TC:** I think Phil would very willingly acknowledge John Coltrane as an influence.

ST: Would that jazz influence account for Phil's approach to bass playing, which is very different from other rock bass guitarists?

TC: The sheer force of his creativity can't be contained in four strings.

ST: Was there a component of the drug experience that had an impact on the band's style of lengthy improvisational music?

TC: I'm sure it did. There were those people that were always trying to dose us, and sometimes they succeeded, I'll say that much. There are two things I'd like to point out. One is that the experience varies widely from one person to another and, secondly, the perception is necessarily different for the listener than it is for the performer — even when they're the same person. There is a wide variety of possibilities when it comes to psychedelics. I remember one time when the band got rather heavily dosed and it seemed like the instruments were painted onto you.

ST: Do you recall the period of time when *Live Dead* was recorded?

TC: This was about the time we were finishing up the work on the *Aoxomoxoa* project and Warner Brothers was pointing out to us that they had sunk one hundred thousand plus dollars into it and hadn't seen a product yet. So someone had the idea that if we sent them a double live album, three discs for that price wouldn't be such a bad deal, and they went for it. So we started sixteen-track taping every show. That weekend when *Live Dead* was recorded was the first one where no one raised an objection to the performances. We were hoping that one of the ones along the line would be okay at least and, at the time, we figured that they weren't objectionable — not that they were excellent. As I recall, shortly after that period of time with that pressure off, the band started to play even better.

ST: The improvisational playing and the energy from that period is just remarkable.

TC: There were times when the band liked to try something different. Jerry, especially, would get an idea of something that would go out of something and he would try it out. That's another aspect. There's perhaps a more rough-cut flavor or texture to the music but, at the same time, more adventurous and exciting because we'd try things.

ST: Where did the feedback passages develop from?

**TC:** It was your mammoth bringing of a plane in for a landing at the end of a huge jam. A guitar solo would naturally lead into feedback because you're pushing it for its last ounce of explosive power.

**ST:** Was Bear mixing sound in those days?

**TC:** That was the pretext for traveling with the band. Healy would help with the knobs when people got fed up with the Bear. Pigpen described the system as one that worked 100% well, 20% of the time.

**ST:** Do you recall when the band performed "Hey Jude?"

**TC:** Yes, Pigpen was doing the vocal. We learned to do it at the Fillmore East. It was rare for the band to do any Beatles material at all and we didn't do "Hey Jude" very often either.

**ST:** Wasn't Pigpen the front man for the band in the '60s, doing mostly blues tunes?

**TC:** Pigpen's father was a blues DJ who went by the name "Cool Breeze." Pigpen had an encyclopedic knowledge of all the blues artists and Pigpen was a remarkable blues singer. The world never got to see the full measure of Pigpen. He could do so many things — he was so deep, so broad. I used to room with him on the road and I shared a house with him in Novato. I mean you'd look at him and see this Hell's Angel sort of character who sings this narrow band of music and he was really into so many more things. Pigpen had a different outer and inner image. While his outer image was kind of like Pirate Pete who would shoot his gun at your feet to make you dance, yet he was also the guy who brought a portable chess game along on the road because he liked to play.

**ST:** His style of singing songs like "Lovelight" or "Midnight Hour" lent itself to a lot of vocal improvisation.

**TC:** He was very natural at it.

**ST:** Pigpen and Janis Joplin seemed like kindred spirits. For instance, both sang the blues and knew how to get the most out of a song.

**TC:** Definitely, in many ways. Pigpen proudly claimed he turned her on to Southern Comfort.

**ST:** Didn't Janis sit in with the Dead at the Fillmore West and share vocals with Pigpen on "Lovelight?"

**TC:** I remember them doing that.

**ST:** Do you particularly remember any outstanding shows from that era when you were in the band?

TC: Most any show at the Fillmore East was exceptional. The Fillmore East was a magical place to play — the crowd was very responsive. The band had a strong following in New York and it put an edge on the playing. I'd rather listen to any "Dark Star" from the Fillmore East. They were in a different class.

ST: Do you remember any other groups jamming with the band?

TC: I remember a San Diego show where Santana sat in with us at San Diego State. Also, the New Orleans Pop Festival where the Jefferson Airplane sat in with us. There was also one time at a place on Sunset Boulevard called Thelma's, right next to the Whiskey A Go-Go, where Stephen Stills and David Crosby sat in with us. All these interactions and musical culture bouncing off each other were a lot of fun.

ST: You mentioned musical culture bouncing off each other. It seems the Dead has always had an affinity for Bob Dylan.

TC: It was like a kindred expression. Although I don't see Dylan as a necessary influence to Hunter's lyrics, he thinks highly of him.

ST: What was Woodstock like?

TC: As I recall, I was the only one in the band that had a good time, and even that was mitigated because everyone else wasn't. The guitarists were getting shocked from their strings. Bob described his strings as being like barbed wire. The electricity wasn't grounded. It was supposed to be on a circular stage and we were supposed to spin and come on as we were playing but our equipment was too heavy. It didn't work. The stage was swaying back and forth. Phil was visualizing the headlines the next day reading, "Huge Rock and Roll Disaster — Thousands Maimed."

JIM MARSHALL

The Grateful Dead at Yasgur's Farm, August 16, 1969

**ST:** After you left the band at the end of January 1970, didn't you make a guest appearance at the Fillmore East in 1971?

**TC:** On April 28, 1971 I sat in with them. I was in New York finishing up the recording of *Tarot*. I didn't even go to the Fillmore East with the idea of playing. I just went to visit Pigpen and the others. I was backstage at the Fillmore East and the next thing I knew I was sitting down at the keyboard. I was just along for the ride.

**ST:** That jam was a delight. ("Dark Star" into "St. Stephen" into "Not Fade Away" into "Going Down the Road" into "Not Fade Away.")

**TC:** It gives you the feeling like pieces of a jigsaw puzzle popping into place, very serendipitously.

**ST:** How did the Grateful Dead reflect the consciousness of the '60s?

**TC:** It was like Camelot. I felt like I couldn't possibly appreciate it enough at the time. Here you are at the oasis and you are just drinking yourself drunk. Florence, Phil's old lady at the time, describes being in the Grateful Dead extended family as like living on a block where all the kids were like you.

**ST:** How large was the Grateful Dead family in those days?

**TC:** Once, at Phil's house, we had a band meeting and realized we had five managers, the duties of all of which we didn't even know. It was pretty loose.

**ST:** It seems like it was more than coincidence that you guys ended up in the Grateful Dead playing music together.

**TC:** Henry Miller said coincidence is a word for order that we haven't understood.

AMANDA VASKAS

## JOHN "MARMADUKE" DAWSON

Marmaduke was the founder of the New Riders of the Purple Sage, a country rock band that originally consisted of David Nelson on guitar, Jerry Garcia on pedal steel guitar, Phil Lesh on bass, Mickey Hart on drums, and Dawson on rhythm guitar and vocals. In 1970 as part of "An Evening with the Grateful Dead" the New Riders opened the show and the Dead then played an acoustic set and a lengthy electric set.

ST: How did you meet Jerry Garcia?

JD: If you were a guitar picker of any kind in Palo Alto you started knowing who the other guitar players were. I got into that scene back in 1958-59 when I first started taking guitar lessons from a lady in Palo Alto. Jerry was living with Sarah then. They had a little duet called Jerry and Sarah, and Garcia would play the mandolin and Sarah would play the guitar and sing. They played around in little coffee houses and folk spots. They dropped in at a guitar thing that my guitar teacher was having at her house one night. I didn't really meet him until later on at a club called the Tangent in downtown Palo Alto. They had hootenannies, or open-mike nights as they call them these days, on Wednesday nights and lots of people would go down there and hang out to meet people. I think I first met David Nelson at that spot. A lot of the people that are in the Dead scene got to know each other in the early days in Palo Alto. There was another coffee house that didn't particularly have a lot of music in it, but people hung out there a lot, called Saint Michael's Alley. Another place where people hung out and chewed the fat and got to know each other was Keplers Bookstore in Menlo Park. Joan Baez and Ira Sandperl were known for hanging out there and getting to know each other at that particular place.

Ira Sandperl is an old Palo Alto activist, part-time school teacher, part-time guru, part-time inspirationalist. An interesting sort of fellow. He's the guy who was responsible for a lot of Joan Baez' political leanings. A lot of the political stuff can be traced somewhat to Ira Sandperl. He used to come over and teach literature classes where I went to school at a place called the Peninsula School in Palo Alto. So lots of scenes were interconnected back in those days.

ST: This was during the folk music period?

JD: The part of the folk music period that I got to be a part of was during the period from 1959 to 1963 when I got to know all those people.

ST: Were you aware of those configurations of groups that Jerry was in, like the Wildwood Boys?

JD: That was one of those early configurations. He was playing banjo.

ST: There was the Thunder Mountain Tub Stumpers and the Hart Valley Drifters. Those were in 1963 and 1964.

JD: Those are all various aggregations of people who got to-

gether for one or two gigs and just decided to call themselves some weird name that they had come up with on the
tradition of those weird old names that people used to have
for their bands.

ST: One of the early configurations was Jerry, Pigpen, and Bob
Weir in a jug band.

JD: They had a jug band called Mother McRee's Uptown Jug
Champions and that's the one that was the last configuration
of a jug band before they started up with the Warlocks.

ST: Do you recall when the Warlocks started playing?

JD: Yes, I was hanging out in the summer of 1965 when the
Warlocks first starting playing. They had Dana Morgan on
the bass because he was the guy that owned the music shop
that was supplying all the instruments for them. He turned
out not to be a very good bass player and they had to get
rid of him. Jerry remembered he had this old friend, Phil
Lesh, who was hanging out up in San Francisco and was an
excellent musician although he hadn't played any bass. He
called him up and said, "Hey, we need a bass player. Come
on down." And so he came down and took up the job. They
started playing in the pizza place in Menlo Park during that
summer of 1965, I believe.

ST: Was that Magoo's Pizza Parlor?

JD: Yes. They were the Warlocks when they were playing in
that place. As the Warlocks they also played at this other
club in San Mateo for a while called The Fireside. I heard
them a couple of times there. That was in the days when
Pigpen was playing a lot of blues harmonica and they were
trying to be a white blues band.

ST: Pigpen's influence was certainly appreciated by a lot of fans.

JD: He did some good shots. He was a good organ player too.

ST: 1965 was about the time when Kesey was starting to do the
Acid Tests.

JD: Right. The first Acid Test was in 1965. I was at a lot of them.
You can tell a lot of the changes that came on with the arrival
of LSD on the West Coast in the spring of 1965. Things got
loose. After they got their first record contract, I would go
and hang out with them at 710 Ashbury Street. It was a
good scene.

ST: Were you part of any of the scenes at the ranch in Marin?

JD: A bunch of the Dead went up and lived at this place called

Rancho Olompali. It's up near Novato. It's a place where the Indians used to hang out. There is an Indian burial ground nearby. It's quite a lovely place. It had a big old mansion of a ranch house that they lived in for a while.

ST: When did you start getting seriously involved with music?

JD: That wasn't until the spring of 1969. I went with a bunch of guys down to a place called Pinnacle's National Monument, which is south of the Bay Area, and a group of us ate a bunch of what we thought was mescaline but was some weird little chemical cocktail that had some LSD in it. I had an experience on that particular occasion and I made up my mind that I wanted to write songs more seriously and learn how to sing more seriously. I liked the idea of being a country-western singer and started picking up Buck Owen and Merle Haggard records to try to learn how they were doing it. I had this idea because I loved the pedal steel guitar. I thought it would be a neat thing for a band, which was more country-western oriented than the Dead were turning out to be. I liked how the Rolling Stones tried to do American country songs but I didn't think that they gave them enough country flavor. I wanted to use that bluegrass harmony with the Rolling Stones type of punch and let the other guys play along with it. That old bluegrass idea where one guy takes this break and another guy takes that break and you sing harmony on the chorus.

The New Riders came along in 1969 when Mickey Hart had his ranch up in Novato. We used to practice in the barn. There was a horse living beneath where we were practicing. We set the band up on this thing that looked like a stage but was the roof over the horse's stall. We set the band equipment up there and improvised a little P.A. system.

ST: Who was in the first configuration of the New Riders?

JD: Hunter was going to try to be the bass player for a while but he didn't have that many chops together. Bob Matthews tried out but he wasn't able to pick up on the instrument quickly enough because all of the rest of us had been playing for a long time. That's when Phil Lesh finally stepped in and played bass with the New Riders. David Nelson was our guitar player. What had happened is that I invited myself over to Garcia's house one day after he had come back off the road with a brand-new pedal steel guitar. He had stopped in Denver at a music store that had a bunch of pedal steels in it. So he bought one and brought it back. I

David Nelson

bumped into him at the Dead's practice place in Novato near Hamilton Air Force Base. I asked Jerry if I could come over to his house and listen to the steel guitar that he just bought. He said I could come over later if I wanted to hear it. I brought my guitar when I showed up so he would have something to accompany. I showed him a couple of tunes that I had been working on and I got to listen to the pedal steel. That little duet worked into a thing where Jerry asked me if he could come down and practice his pedal steel at my coffee house gig in Menlo Park. I think it was called The Underground and it was a hofbrau kind of thing where they would carve you up a sandwich from a fresh cut of meat, right on the spot.

ST:  So Jerry came down and jammed with you?

JD:  Jerry came down and set his steel up and accompanied what I was doing, building up his chops. It sounded good. Pretty soon we had kids coming down every week. We did it for several weekends during the summer of 1969. There was a pizza parlor up the street that normally had all the kids in it. But about 7:00 p.m. on Wednesday evenings they would all come down the street to the Underground for Jerry and my performance. It was kind of interesting. I think I still have a tape of one of our performances.

ST:  You thought it sounded pretty good so you guys decided to build on it?

JD:  Yes. That's exactly what happened. We were having fun doing it so it gave us the idea to have a country-western honky-tonk band. We needed a guitar player so David Nelson joined us. He was living with what was left of Big

The Grateful Dead & the New Riders at Mickey's Barn, Novato, California

Brother and the Holding Company after Janis left. They had a warehouse and he was living in it up in San Francisco. He came down and we started rehearsing some good old country-western favorites and some of my songs. Then we got Mickey Hart to drum. That's how we came to practice up in his barn a little later on. First it was Bob Hunter on the bass for a day or so and then it was Bob Matthews and then it was Phil.

The configuration of the band was Mickey Hart on the drums, Phil Lesh on the bass, me on the rhythm guitar and most of the lead vocals, Garcia on the steel, and David Nelson on the lead guitar and some of the vocals.

**ST:** Did you guys do any local gigs?

**JD:** We gigged around for a while. We did all sorts of songs. We were quite eclectic. After a while it got to be that they just added Nelson and me to the Grateful Dead tour and we came along with them that way. That's when we first got started on the national scene and you heard us back there in 1970 on the East Coast at the Fillmore — "An Evening with the Grateful Dead featuring the New Riders of the Purple Sage."

**ST:** That was a great period for the Grateful Dead.

**JD:** That's when you only had to add Nelson's and my ticket to the tour and you had a whole new five-piece band to open, which made it quite handy. That got my songs exposed to a national audience a lot sooner than they would have been otherwise. We also had a gospel quartet that did some stuff. Nelson would play an acoustic and Bob Weir, Jerry, and I would come out and would sing a couple of gospel tunes.

**ST:** What did you think of the Fillmore East?

**JD:** That was quite a flash. I had been on stage before in front of people but that particular setup with their excellent sound system was really quite an impressive thing for someone who had never seen something like that before.

**ST:** The first album you did had Dave Torbert on bass.

**JD:** Right. Dave Torbert was a friend of Nelson's. They had been in another band for a while called the New Delhi River Band. Torbert had been the bass player in that band. Phil at some point said, "Hey, I don't want to do it any more." So that's when David Torbert joined the band.

**ST:** Did you write all the songs on that album?

**JD:** Yes. I had been collecting them for a while. They didn't all come at once but I wrote them all and that was my little song bag. It's still a record that I'm proud of.

**ST:** It's well-deserved.

**JD:** Well, thanks. What is really a flash is that some other musicians think enough of them to be doing them.

**ST:** Those songs certainly seem to fit well within the whole "Evening with the Grateful Dead" concept.

**JD:** That was intended. Like I said, I wanted to do something with the improvisational qualities that they had but was a little bit more standardized. I wasn't much into the long spacey jams and that stuff.

**ST:** Jerry recounts that he wasn't real happy with his pedal steel playing.

**JD:** He was only comparing himself to other steel guitar players from Nashville, professional pedal steel guitar players of which he would never admit he was one. Although he did one of the best pedal steel tracks of all time on "Teach Your Children."

**ST:** You listen to those songs he plays from that era and he has a distinct style that sounded great. It really blended well with the music.

**JD:** It was breaking new ground for its day too, as a matter of fact. No other pedal steel guitar players would do stuff like that. When we finally met another pedal steel guitar player in the person of Buddy Cage on the ride across Canada in 1970, that gave Garcia a chance to go back to just the Grateful Dead.

**ST:** When you say the ride across Canada, was that the infamous trans-Canadian train tour?

**JD:** I don't know why you say "infamous" but yes, it was fun. There was a whole train load full of musicians. It was called Festival Express, 1970.

**ST:** Who was there?

**JD:** The Band was supposed to be on it but the only person from the Band that actually showed up and rode the train was Rick Danko. And then there was Ian and Sylvia's band. That was how we found Buddy Cage. The Grateful Dead and New Riders, of course. The Guess Who from Canada, Delaney and Bonnie, Mountain with Leslie West the guitar player, and Janis Joplin and her band.

**ST:** So where did the train go?

**JD:** The train went from Toronto to Winnepeg and Calgary. There was a restaurant car and two club cars. There were several cars where everybody was sleeping, the European convertible types where people sit during the day and they become a sleeper at night.

**ST:** That must have been pretty wild.

**JD:** It was wild and it was a lot of fun. We played three big shows and ended up rolling all the way across Canada. The train was about to run out of booze on the day after we left Winnepeg and the day before we got into Calgary. After a while there was no more CC left, no more tequila, and no more nothing. This was getting serious so a bunch of self-appointed committee members went running around the place taking up a collection. "Hey, the train ran out of booze and we're coming into Saskatoon in a minute and there will be a chance to restock so give us some money right now." So these people went up and down the length of the train asking for money and they ended up with about four hundred bucks. Back in 1970 that was a considerable amount of money and liquor. So they jumped into a taxicab the second the train arrived in Saskatoon, and rode it for several miles into town. They parked our rock and roll train at a separate station out of town rather than the main train station in town, I guess, because they didn't want to contaminate their citizenry. But anyway they ran into town and the story I heard was that they arrived at this liquor store and plunked the $400 down on the table top and said, "Here's $400, tell us when we've reached it," and they started grabbing stuff off the shelf. And they ended up with this $400 booze run. They put it all back into the taxicab and hauled it all the way back to the train. Of course there was only going to be one more night on the train anyway so we had to drink it all that night. As I recollect, there was this three-foot-tall bottle of Canadian Club around which Buddy Cage was found wrapped the next morning. It was quite an interesting night with Janis Joplin and Jerry Garcia. It's the first and last time I ever saw Jerry high on liquor. As I recollect, he took a couple of pulls on the tequila bottle that night. Rick Danko and Janis sat around improvising on "No More Cane on the Brazos." It ran on for about thirty minutes and each verse was funnier than the last one.

**ST:** Was Jerry singing with them?

**JD:** Jerry was singing a little bit too.

**ST:** One of the legendary shows is Harpur College in May of 1970.

**JD:** The famous SUNY Binghamton show. The thing about that show was at least two-thirds of the audience was stoned out of their minds on LSD at the time. It was their own mini-version of the Acid Test, as close as they could reproduce it. There they were in the gym quite ready for the music. It was a good evening.

**ST:** Eventually Spencer Dryden joined the band as a drummer.

**JD:** That happened about the time we started to make the records.

**ST:** Where was that picture taken that is on the back of the first album?

**JD:** That's the house in Kentfield. It's the house where Hunter brought over the beginning words to "Friend of the Devil" and I came up with the second phrase.

**ST:** In 1971 the New Riders toured with the Dead pretty exclusively.

**JD:** Yes. We did the concerts in Portchester, the famous bomb scare night was one of those I remember. We did all six nights. Howie Stein was the promoter. He painted the stage purple for us. It was the New Riders of the Purple Stage.

**ST:** That's great! Did you go to Europe with the Dead in 1972?

**JD:** *Powerglide*, our second album, was about to come out so when the Dead went to Europe in the spring of '72 we went too. We played with them at a festival called Bickershaw. In the north of England near Manchester. Then we went our separate ways through Europe for about a week or so. We went to Amsterdam and Germany and a couple of places in Britain and the Grateful Dead went and did their thing with the bus tour, the Bozos and the Bolos. We bumped into them again a week or so later when we both played together at the Lyceum in London.

**ST:** Did you play there for four nights?

**JD:** We played all four nights. The Lyceum was an old theater that they had taken all the seats off the floor. The floor was like a dance concert configuration. The box seats were still good on the sides. CBS records had rented one of the boxes for their exclusive use and Warner Brothers Records had rented one of the boxes on the other side for their exclusive use. From these two boxes things kept raining down on the audience. Little samples and gifts that the record companies try to entice the audience with. The CBS people in London had this round logo representing the first record and they were also giving away stickers. The Grateful Dead people on the other side were also giving away stickers and all sorts of stuff.

**ST:** Do you recall the concert where the New Riders were playing at the Felt Forum in March of 1973 and some of the Dead dropped in and played with you?

**JD:** That was a nice fat evening. It was a really fun night. We got Jerry and Bobby to come and help us. Jerry played banjo on some tunes and Bobby was playing acoustic guitar.

**ST:** Another album the New Riders did was *Panama Red*.

**JD:** That was the album that went gold for us. Peter Rowan wrote the song "Panama Red" and was doing it with Old And In The Way. David Grisman was playing the mandolin, Jerry was playing banjo, Peter was playing guitar, John Kahn on bass, and Richard Green on fiddle. Owsley was recording them. Jerry kept up his interest in country music that way. He's a picking junkie, first and foremost. He would rather be playing than anything else.

**ST:** How would you classify your music?

**JD:** You can call it country rock. I always called it country flavor rock and roll but that's too many words.

**ST:** It seems like the Grateful Dead were sort of in sync with what you were doing.

**JD:** You've got to remember that we are all former folk musicians. We are all people who formerly hung around coffee houses and hootenannies and stuff like that. So it would be more logical for us to go in that direction.

MICHAEL ZAGARIS

175

## STANLEY MOUSE

Stanley Mouse has been described by Bill Graham as one of the definitive '60s people. A prolific artist who was one of the original poster artists from Haight-Ashbury, Mouse and his former partner Alton Kelley created many of the classic Grateful Dead posters and album covers.

**ST:** How did you become an artist?

**SM:** My father was an artist and he worked for Walt Disney in the 1930s and early '40s. I was born in California and when the war started, our family moved back east. Being in Detroit, I was interested in cars. When I was old enough to drive I started to flame, pinstripe, and paint pictures on cars. Then I got hold of an airbrush and started to paint t-shirts. From the day I painted my first t-shirt, nobody would leave me alone. People would just badger me for an airbrushed t-shirt. So I set up a booth at the local drag strip and the State fair and started painting shirts. Then I put an ad in some of the national hot-rod magazines and started getting a lot of orders. I was 18 or 19 then and I was making the equivalent of $1,000 a week, and sometimes more, painting t-shirts and selling them. Then I would go out on weekends to hot-rod shows around the East Coast, and I'd make a couple thousand extra at the car show. During the week I actually went to art school. This went on for about eight years where I went to art school on and off, painted t-shirts, and had this giant company going. My family helped me with it.

**ST:** What was the name of it?

**SM:** Mouse Studios. I got the name "Mouse" in grade school probably because I was quiet and drew pictures and cartoons a lot.

**ST:** What brought you back to California?

**SM:** The evolvement in my art that came about through the psychedelic movement took me away from the hot-rod scene and into something else that seemed to be happening around me. Being from California originally, I yearned to get back there. With Vietnam happening and big attitudinal and social changes taking place — the peace movement, civil rights, Bob Dylan, Joan Baez, etc. — things were bristling, and Berkeley seemed to be a real hot spot for my drawings and cartoons that portrayed LBJ and anti-war themes.

I moved to Berkeley in 1964 and lived in this little windmill on Telegraph Avenue. I set up my airbrush and started painting t-shirts.

I left California in 1965 because I got drafted and had to go back to Detroit. I got out of the draft by the skin of my teeth and then I got a drive-away car to come back to California. The only vehicle going to California was a hearse. I thought that was perfect because I could get all my stuff in it. So I slapped a "Make love not war" sticker on the hearse, put my lady and dog in the back with all my supplies, and came out to California in January 1966. I pulled into San Francisco the night of the Trips Festival and ended up in front of the Longshoremen's Hall — it was amazing timing.

**ST:** When did you start doing the concert posters?

**SM:** The first one I did was a Family Dog poster for a Captain Beefheart concert in June of 1966. Then Kelley and I started working together and we did a collaboration, the "Zig Zag Man" for a Big Brother concert.

**ST:** How many posters did you do for the Family Dog?

**SM:** Right after I did the "Zig Zag Man," I started a whole run of posters. Just about every week Kelley and I did a poster for the Family Dog. We did thirty or forty posters in about a year.

**ST:** How did psychedelics affect the '60's poster art?

**SM:** The use of psychedelics really enhanced the visual experience.

**ST:** It seems that the posters were a reflection of the psyche-delic experience.

**SM:** I don't know if they reflected everything, but they were highly influenced by it.

**ST:** Some of the psychedelic drugs like window-pane acid were very visual.

**SM:** Sure. The Grateful Dead movie showed that.

**ST:** You mean the animation?

**SM:** Yes. The animation of Gary Gutierrez. He really did pin down what the inner vision of the mind does, but that's only with your eyes closed. When your eyes are open it's a different story.

**ST:** How did you get involved with the Grateful Dead?

**SM:** Well, they were one of the bands that played the Avalon. Of course, they were one of the most fun bands to do a poster for because of their name.

**ST:** Did you hang out at the Grateful Dead house at 710 Ashbury?

**SM:** Well, I would go over there once in a while for little get-togethers.

I got a place at 715 Ashbury, across the street from 710 Ashbury, and I moved my studio there. The Dead rented

we did it that it was really hot because it felt right. It just fit so good with the name. The skeleton that symbolized death and the roses that symbolized rebirth and love. It just said Grateful Dead.

ST:  Bill Graham was quoted as saying that you are one of the definitive '60s people. You were right there in the center of it all. What was it like?

SM:  Well, it's true, I did feel very much in the center of the whole thing. But there were also thousands of other people in the center. I had this shop that was probably one of the first head shops and we sold all kinds of stuff — hippie trappings, posters, t-shirts, East Indian imports such as blankets and jewelry, and whatever crafts people would bring in and put on consignment. It was real bizarre. A lot of times there would be parades up and down Haight Street for celebrations and things. When that happened, we would close the doors and line chairs up inside the shop and sit down and watch the parade go by. Because of the windows, anything said just outside the windows would be magnified inside the shop. You could hear anything anyone said as they passed by. They couldn't see inside because the lights would be off during the day. It was like our own little private viewing stand for all the crazy little things that happened.

One time late in the year when the store was really on the wing, people would come in and ask what we sold because they couldn't find anything to buy. There wasn't anything in there! It was going downhill so we went out and bought about ten gallons of bright enamel paint, really bright, and we had all these artists come in and paint murals all over the inside of the place. This one speed-freak artist just kept painting and painting, and what started out as bright psychedelic colors ended up kind of brown because he painted over the top of everybody's murals.

ST:  Living in Haight-Ashbury you had a chance to meet some interesting people. I understand you were good friends with Janis Joplin.

SM:  I really liked Janis; she was a lot of fun, to say the least. We always hung out together backstage. We hung out with the same people so we saw a lot of each other.

ST:  Do you have any good stories about Janis?

SM:  I knew James Gurley, the lead guitarist for Big Brother, because we're both from Detroit. Big Brother used to practice at my house (an abandoned firehouse), and one day Janis Joplin came for an audition. Right after the audition, the band came up to me and said, "What do you think, Stanley, what do you think? What did you think of her?" And I said, "She's either really great, or really bad." That night after her audition, two policemen came to the house. They knocked on the door and I opened it up and said, "What do you want?" They said, "We've got reports here of a woman screaming."

ST: How did the light show scene get started?

SM: Well, I think Bill Ham is the one who actually created the light show. He used to have a place near where the Dog House was happening on Pine Street in 1966. His place was around the corner and he had light shows in it. He would have James Gurley come in and play guitar, trippy guitar, and he would do this wild light show, and everybody would come and get high off of the combination of music and lights.

At the time, light shows were nonexistent. They were just starting. What he would do was liquid lights. It would be a dance of color and abstraction. He would have musicians come in and play rock and roll to a blend of the light. The place would only hold 10-15 people. It was a real high experience.

ST: What happened to the Haight-Ashbury scene?

SM: What happened is all the crazies joined in on the trip and brought it to an end. It was a wonderful scene of artists, writers, and musicians. When the media picked up on Haight-Ashbury and broadcast it all over the country, all the crazies jumped in their cars and rushed to the Haight and destroyed it. Otherwise it might have gone on for another three or four years.

ST: After the Haight scene fizzled, didn't the Dead move to Marin?

SM: The Dead had this place up on 101, this big ranch, and they had parties up there. They had a swimming pool and everybody would come to these parties and take their clothes off. They were outrageous parties, really far out. You would be laying around there nude, and all of these people would be jumping in the pool and taking acid.

ST: Where did you go after you left Haight-Ashbury?

SM: I went to England.

**ST:** How long did you live there?

**SM:** I stayed there for a year. I worked on the Blind Faith album cover and did some work for the Beatles.

**ST:** What kind of work did you do for the Beatles?

**John Lennon, Yoko Ono & Stanley Mouse, the Amsterdam 'Bed-In for Peace'**

**SM:** I did some small graphic things, a press book cover, nothing major. I originally went to England to flame Eric Clapton's Rolls-Royce but he smashed it up before I got there. I was sitting at home in San Francisco meditating one day and my friend, Bob Seidemann, had gone to England and I was thinking about it. About this time the phone rings and the voice said, "Hello, Stanley, this is Eric Clapton." I said, "Eric, what's happening?" I had met him once when he came to San Francisco. And he said, "How would you like to come to London and flame my Rolls-Royce?" And I said, "Sounds groovy." When he heard me say "groovy" he laughed. When I got there, Eric had just smashed his Rolls-Royce. Some Iranian had run into it and bounced off and then into the Iranian Embassy. I got there the night of the birthday party, when the Beatles sang "It's Your Birthday," the night of George Harrison's girlfriend's birthday party.

ST: Did you work on the cover of *Workingman's Dead*?

SM: I took the photograph and did all the graphics.

ST: Where was the photograph taken?

SM: It was down by the rendering plants by Barney's Beanery in San Francisco. It was hot, about 100 degrees and the band was uncomfortable and that added to the downtrodden, working-class feeling of the photograph.

ST: That was a landmark album.

SM: A lot of people say that *Workingman's Dead* was their best record.

ST: How did Monster Company come about?

SM: Kelley and I started Monster Company, a t-shirt company in San Rafael. We wanted to do four-color process t-shirts, which had never been done before—the four-color process that they use to print photographs and books. Everybody said we couldn't do it. Because of our graphic expertise, we knew it could be done. We went to Ripoff Press and there was a guy printing t-shirts there that didn't know it couldn't be done. We made the four-color screens and took them in there and said, "Here, print this," and it came out. Then we got our own equipment and started to print t-shirts. We refined the four-color process with the help of Robert Tree. At the time we had a really good situation with the Dead. We used nothing but the very best quality shirts and the best printing. It was a superior product. Today the shirts are legendary.

ST: You did the "Blue Rose" poster, which was the poster for the closing of Winterland with the Grateful Dead, the NRPS, and the Blues Brothers.

SM: I remember that I was on stage watching the Grateful Dead and I was next to Dan Aykroyd. I said, "Hey, Dan, how did you like that poster I did for the event?" And he said, "My mother would really like it." And to this day I've always wanted to say I've got something your mother would like.

There was a great party at the Jefferson Airplane house. Everybody was carousing from room to room. Belushi was telling jokes. It was fun meeting him and some of the other *Saturday Night* people.

ST: I understand you lived in New Mexico for a couple of years.

SM: Santa Fe, New Mexico, on Canyon Road. I had a studio gallery where I painted and sold a lot of my paintings. I held

**ST:** What are you currently doing with your art?

**SM:** I have a small storefront gallery studio in Sonoma that I am using as a showcase for my work. I have a lot of landscapes and figurative work mixed in with some of my rock and roll Grateful Dead stuff.

I had these two paintings in my studio and a dear friend of mine, Nicki Scully, brought Mountain Girl over to my house and then we went to my studio. Mountain Girl saw these two paintings that I did in Santa Fe and really liked them. One was a petroglyph of a mountain having a vision of these Indian symbols. The other was the Hopi rain dance of a Hopi Katchina Head. Above it was an eagle with snakes, and at the bottom was a canyon with a petroglyph on its horse, jumping across the canyon. She bought them and took them home and hung them in her dining room. Jerry hadn't even seen them. It gives me a glow to think about these symbolic paintings working on Jerry's subconscious.

**ST:** Stanley, it seems that your art work is quite varied.

**SM:** When I moved to Santa Fe, New Mexico, I submerged myself in oil painting. I did a lot of paintings and studied with other painters. Then I moved to Lake Tahoe for a few years and painted there. I didn't do much commercial work at all. Since I've moved to Sonoma I've been going in all kinds of directions at once. I've been doing oil paintings. I formed a group of painters and we hire a model and do drawings and paintings every week. I go out and do landscape paintings, and still-life paintings. I've been doing fine art reproductions of my art work using the medium of silk-screen serigraphs. Most of them are signed, limited editions. I've also been doing book covers. I just finished a book cover for the *Grateful Dead Family Album* and I did the book cover for your book.

**ST:** What is it about the Grateful Dead that makes them popular today?

**SM:** The Grateful Dead were a phenomenon in Haight-Ashbury in their time, and they kept playing while the scene changed. The kids kept coming and they needed someone to look up to and the Dead still encompassed the philosophy of the '60s — ecology, taking care of the land, and treating people right. The Dead are still here and they're still doing it while many of the other bands have disappeared. Dead Heads are a special part of the human race who are trying to keep alive all of those wonderful qualities of the '60s.

MICHAEL ZAGARIS

## NICKI SCULLY

Nicki Scully has been part of the Dead scene since the '60s when she met Rock Scully, her former husband. Nicki went to Egypt with the Dead when they played at the pyramids in 1978. Since that time she has traveled to Egypt many times and has studied and teaches the Egyptian mysteries. Nicki currently lectures and conducts workshops called the Cauldron Teachings. She leads metaphysical tours to receive initiations in Egypt, has produced three audio tapes, one including music by Jerry Garcia, and is writing a book.

**ST:** How did you meet Rock Scully?

**NS:** At the end of 1966 I was drawn to San Francisco by my interest in mind expansion and, as a result, I wound up dropping into the San Francisco scene. In 1967 I met Rock Scully who was the manager of the Grateful Dead. Rock and I always had an affinity for one another and we got together in 1969 when he was living at the ranch in Novato. Billy Kreutzmann had a tepee set up there and I remember David Crosby and Steven Stills singing and jamming in his tepee. That's where a lot of the influence came from for the harmonies on *Workingman's Dead* and *American Beauty*.

**ST:** Did you go to Woodstock?

**NS:** Yes, it was an incredible event and an extraordinary experience. I ran into the band on the flight to New York by coincidence. Rock wasn't there yet so I went in with Jerry by limo the first day. By the next day the band had to use helicopters to get in. It was such an overwhelming experience to be there with all those people. It kept swelling and kept growing. We were there until after the Dead played and then we left for New York.

**ST:** Another outstanding event was the concert near Eugene, Oregon, in August 1972.

**NS:** That was a benefit for Chuck and Sue Kesey's creamery. Chuck is Ken Kesey's brother and he has a creamery that makes Nancy's Yogurt and other wonderful dairy products.

Nobody expected 25,000 people to show up for that concert. What I remember the most is the view from the stage, looking out on the audience, as the sun was setting. The light behind the hair of all the people in the audience, and their naked bodies. It was so hot that day that nobody could keep their clothes on. It was incredibly hot. But it was also one of the highest and most joyous concerts that I remember experiencing. It was beautiful. There was lots of dancing and joy, just pure joy.

**ST:** As I recall from seeing the movie *Sunshine Daydream* the band played an incredible "Dark Star" as the sun was setting.

**NS:** It was amazing. I'll never forget that one. In my mind's eye I can still see that. I also seem to remember some parachutists. The field that the band was playing on was so large that while they were playing at one end, some skydivers parachuted in at the other end of the field. It was beautiful.

**ST:** Didn't the Dead play at that same site in 1982?

JIM MARSHALL

JG at Woodstock

**NS:** Yes, it was called the Field Trip. It was the Second Decadanel, in 1982, ten years later, on the same site, but with the stage at the opposite end of the meadow from where it was in 1972 so that as the sun was setting you could see the eyes of the band. I established the link that got the concert going. The Field Trip took me about a year and a half to set up. I set about to find out how the band could do it with the Oregon Country Faire.

**ST:** What is the Oregon Country Faire?

**NS:** The Oregon Country Faire was probably the original prototype of the Renaissance Faire but it never sold out to commercialism. It's been going on for twenty years outside of Eugene in Veneta. It's an incredible happening. The Oregon Country Faire is a craft fair where several thousand people come together every July and camp in these beautiful woods along a river and display exquisite handcrafted items — all sorts of things. There is a community village and a place where environmental issues can be expressed and talked about. There's just all kinds of things happening. For three days, it's a city with no electricity, except for the main stage, where people live in incredible harmony. It's a delight to experience — whether you come in during the day as the public does, to walk around and see the sights and buy things, and enjoy the wonderful entertainment — or whether you camp there, like I do every year, to enjoy the party.

**ST:** I understand that the Grateful Dead helped purchase the land where the fair is held.

**NS:** The Dead paid the fair something like $25,000 to have the concert on that land. It wasn't meant to be a benefit but it turned out that way. The Oregon Country Faire was able to get their land which was wonderful.

**ST:** What was the Field Trip like?

**NS:** The wonderful thing about the Second Decadenal was the blend of energy that was mixed with the Oregon Country Faire. It had a special quality the way it was set up. It had a down-home, festive, joyous feeling to it that is not generated by any other mix of energies that come together in a concert.

David Lindquist, the guy who does the native American t-shirts, painted a scrim which surrounded the stage which had the symbols of the northwest Indian on it. It was beautiful. We also had tie-dyed parachutes strung across the field. The food booths were wonderful, with different kinds of food that are not normally available when you go to concerts. Talk about a feast, we really had a good backstage scene. We made this a real party and because there's so much family in Oregon, we wanted it to be a family party.

I particularly enjoyed the fact that Bill Graham came as a guest. I went to the airport to pick him up. It was really fun to bring him into a scene that we had created all by ourselves, without any help from him, and have him go out and enjoy it, which he never gets to do at his own shows, because he's always part of the creative process. You can never experience that in which you are involved in the same way you would if you were a guest. It was great fun to be able to provide that kind of opportunity and have him be willing to come and play. I really enjoyed that.

ST: Why don't we talk about the Grateful Dead family notion.

NS: To me, I always felt as though that family, as ambiguous as it was, was equally strong in ties as my blood family. Just now I'm beginning to understand the depths of my relationship to my other family. I had to leave it to learn to value it and that space of time was filled with the Grateful Dead. The Grateful Dead was a life experience ... the center of our existence. It was this incredible involvement, so dynamic, that took up the largest part of our life, in terms of energy and interest. It was a very consuming thing but, at the same time, very giving.

ST: It seems that the band is very supportive of their organization and the people working for them.

NS: They were incredibly supportive. Actually, I am still surviving with the graces of the support that we initially had from the Grateful Dead. Those final concerts of the Grateful Dead in 1974, when they were going on that hiatus, provided homes for at least three of the families — Ramrod's family, Kreutzmann's family, and our family. What was particularly fortunate in our case was that the home we found was given to us in a rather unconventional manner by someone who wasn't that interested in money. So to buy our land in Forestville cost what most anyone else's down payment would be. We were literally given, free and clear, a beautiful ranch in Sonoma County which was paid for through the benefit of those last concerts before the hiatus. It gave us a place to be during that break when there was no Grateful Dead.

ST: That seems like a real nice gesture on behalf of the band.

**NS:** Well, they have always supported their people. It was such an unconventional business. There was nothing conventional about the way the Grateful Dead was run during those years. It was very organic, sort of like an experiment ... an unruly experiment. It had its pitfalls and we all had a lot to learn.

**ST:** I think part of the reason that people are so fanatical about the Grateful Dead is that either on a cognitive level or an intuitive level fans realize there is more to the Grateful Dead than rock and roll music. They represent something beyond just going to see a rock concert.

**NS:** I guess it's because we are all trying to live our vision and make our vision important.

**ST:** Well, as you said, they're not a conventional business organization. It seems they do things to fulfill dreams, like going to Egypt for instance.

**NS:** I thought it was pretty wild and not exactly your best business deal. But that wasn't the motivating part. For me, Egypt was a call that I could not resist. There was this inexorable pull; I had to go to Egypt. There was no way that I could not go to Egypt. I remember Mountain Girl suggested that I think of some way to support myself going there, other than to just see the band. So I came up with this idea to go and buy things, all different kinds of things from Egypt, and have an import business and bring back samples from this first excursion. So, meanwhile, Rock was working in the studio, so he couldn't make the charter. The charter was leaving from San Francisco so he gave me his ticket and poor Rock never got to Egypt.

**ST:** What was that charter flight like?

**NS:** Oh, the charter flight was outrageous. There must have been a hundred of us on it, mostly Dead family. I remember Kesey being on it. Most of the family that was on the charter wasn't the actual crew or band. The actual crew went their way, but all of us, the family members, all of the people that were "connected," were able to get this charter. But we didn't have the whole plane, we only had a hundred seats on it. So there's all these other straight tourists on this plane, traveling to Egypt. I mean, there we were in international waters. We let all the rules and all the laws go, and we're smoking up, carrying on, and having our party much to the chagrin and fear of a lot of our fellow passengers. I think the crew handled it okay.

**ST:** So there were Dead Heads on the plane also?

**NS:** There were those that were connected closely enough to have gotten on this charter, but it was mostly family. But how far does it extend? The line between Dead Head and family is kind of fine. You know, I'm a Dead Head. Actually, I started from family and became a Dead Head. That's the way it was for me. But I was always a Dead Head while I was family too. So it was a really fun flight. I'm sure it's the most fun flight I've ever taken anywhere. There was music, and everybody was trying to use up their dope because nobody knew what the border was going to be like so everyone was into whatever they brought for the trip. It was very raucous, fun, joyous, and exciting, in anticipation of what it was going to be like in Egypt. We were embarking on a great adventure and we were into it. The other tourists who were embarking on their own adventure were looking at it a lot differently. So it was a very interesting flight. Then, what happened to me when I hit Egypt was extraordinary. Now, I understand it as a lack of "groundedness." If you're going to fly, if you're going to soar on the magic, you really need to be grounded, because otherwise you're like a feather in the wind. You get lost in it. I was so caught up in the excitement and the magic that I couldn't sleep, I couldn't eat, and I was just moved by the idiosyncrasies of the moment. Every moment, every experience, was imbued with magic at many levels that you could perceive. You could go in and out of it but it was a constant. So my perception over time became altered until I really didn't have a great grasp on what I was doing. Finally, Kesey grabbed me in the hall in the Mena House and he said, you need to go to sleep — you need to go to sleep now. I said, "Oh, no, I have to do this, or that, or whatever." And he took out a Seconal and he put it in my mouth and made me swallow it and made me go to bed. I remember that John Kahn said it was "like children out loose in the world with no parents and no cops." But, fortunately for me, we kind of looked after each other because I was borderline at that point. I had driven myself because I was so entranced by the magic of the place.

**ST:** What was the Mena House like?

**NS:** The Mena House is a beautiful, stately, old Egyptian Hotel. One of the finest hotels in the Middle East, I understand. The Mena House is a very established hotel and the special beauty of it is that it's at the foot of the pyramids. From some of the band members' rooms, you could look out the window and see the pyramids. It was a very well-contained place, with beautiful gardens. It was a very lovely hotel to stay in and it gave you the rest and amenities you needed in a place as rough as Egypt, coming from what we're accustomed to here in the States.

**ST:** What was it like when the entourage of the Dead and family members descended upon the hotel?

**NS:** You have to realize that for thousands of years these megalithic monuments have drawn tourists from all over the world, from all sorts of persuasions, to see them. So they're used to a lot. I will say, however, that this entourage of crazies made a big, definite impression on these people who've seen it all. They loved it. It was different. Our whole approach and attitude was so fresh, by comparison, to what they were accustomed to. We brought t-shirts and they loved the t-shirts. You would see the different Dead images peering out from under the gallabayas.

**ST:** I understand that someone put a Dead flag on top of one of the pyramids.

**NS:** That was George Walker, one of the Pranksters, that actually put the flag up there. I climbed the pyramid one morning before sunrise with a whole bunch of people but I had vertigo so it took me a little longer to climb it. I remember that I was about three-quarters of the way up when the sun first crept up. When I got to the top, there were quite a few of us up there, including Bob Weir.

**ST:** This was the Great Pyramid?

**NS:** Yes, the Great Pyramid. Back then you could only climb it in the night and there's only one corner that you could go up. You could pay a guide to take you up the northeast corner along the cornerstone. Now it's much more restricted and you can only climb the smallest of the three pyramids.

Being at the top of the pyramid looking at the rising of the sun and looking toward Cairo in the distance, across Egypt, across the desert, was quite wondrous. My guide's name was Farad and those of us who met up there climbed down the pyramid and went to Farad's house in the village and his wife cooked us breakfast.

**ST:** How were the concerts?

**NS:** There were three concerts which took place in the evening.

There was a stage at the foot of the temple that's alongside the Sphinx. So the alignment was that the pyramids were the backdrop for the event, to the left was the desert, and behind us was the village. The Sphinx was to the right of the stage. The Sphinx and the pyramids were lit up and an obvious part of the backdrop. The scene was incredible. The sky was cloudless, blanketed with stars. There was a full moon. And on the third night, there was an eclipse of the moon. It was phenomenal, to have a full moon and an eclipse. I believe that this was the night that the Camp David accords were signed, which we always thought was an interesting synchronous event. I remember giving Bob Weir

a crystal and I think he even used it a little bit as a slide for his guitar at one point. I was very much into crystals and sort of foisting that interest on everybody. I think all the band members actually had one while they were playing.

ST: How did Hamza El-Din play?

NS: That's the other exquisite part of this. The shows were opened by Hamza El-Din. Hamza had not been back to Egypt in 25 years, I believe. His family was all present for this occasion. Hamza opened the show and played his oud. Hamza is the foremost person who brought the oud to America and gave it notoriety in the musical world. He was returning to Egypt after all those years so it was a proud moment in his life. He invited his family to perform and they were lined up across the stage doing the hand-clapping song along with Mickey and Billy who were also performing with them. Then, one by one, the remaining band members joined in. Jerry started to play and the remaining band members followed. It was a weaving of the rhythms of Egypt with the culture the band was bringing to Egypt. It just created this incredible tapestry of harmony, alliance, and union. Then slowly the Egyptians receded from the stage leaving the Grateful Dead, in their glory, to continue. It was

just amazing. It was just so exquisitely done, this whole cultural interaction. It was memorable because it touched so many levels. It was artistically exquisite. It also had a lot of meaning with regard to the bringing together of the different cultures.

**ST:** So what was it like the third night when there was a total lunar eclipse?

**NS:** It was very cosmic. It went beyond the music. In the state of consciousness that I was in that third night, I couldn't be a good judge because it all sounded wonderful to me. The

The Grateful Dead in Egypt

magic was so "on" that third night and it was as perfect as you can get, and a little more because the circumstances were so extraordinary.

The people from the village came along the sand to the side of the stage and were dancing in the sand. There wasn't a large audience so the few hundred of us that were there had to generate a lot of energy.

**ST:** Didn't Bill Graham do something special for the band in Egypt?

**NS:** Yes. At the end of the third night Bill hired forty camels and horses to take us across the desert to Sahara City, which was a nightclub that he had reserved for us for a show and breakfast, and to watch the sunrise.

**ST:** What is Sahara City like?

**NS:** It's a nightclub in a tent out in the desert that has great belly dancers and wonderful food. For me, though, getting there was the thing. It was riding the Egyptian Arabian horses! Oh, my God, they were fabulous! Those horses were bred to run in the desert, and because there were people that knew of my love of horses and knew that I could ride, they had saved one for me. I'll never forget that horse. His name was Wahed. It means "The One."

**ST:** How far a ride was it?

**NS:** We rode from the concert site, across the desert, several miles to Sahara City. It was just wonderful, this sense of flying across the desert on these surefooted fast animals that knew what they were doing and lived for those moments, with the moon shining down.

**ST:** What was the feast like at Sahara City?

**NS:** I love the Egyptian food. We were wined and dined in great style. It was quite a banquet and a wonderful way to wind up the adventure.

**ST:** I understand that you went into the King and Queen's chamber in the Great Pyramid?

**NS:** I did a lot of my exploring with Courtenay Pollack, the tie-dye artist who, in the '60s, was doing the speaker faces for the band. He and I talked the guards into letting us into the pit of the Great Pyramid. If you've seen diagrams of the pyramid, you can see there are the chambers above, and there's this lengthy shaft that takes you down to a place that's way below it all. That's where the pit is. Some people call it the chamber of initiation.

It's my belief that the Great Pyramid is not a tomb, but that it's a place of initiation to the mysteries. So the first time we went down there, the guard gave us a stub of a candle. You had to literally crawl down this path and you could see where it changed, when you were no longer in the pyramid itself, but beneath the pyramid in the ground. And you would go deeper, and at the bottom, from that vantage point, if you would look all the way up, you could see light where it opened. It's my understanding that at certain times of the year this shaft gives a direct line to the star Sirius through which the ancients are supposedly connected and can communicate. From the bottom of that shaft it levels out and when you go through the passageway you enter the pit. It's absolutely dark. That little shaft of light did not begin to penetrate the cavern where the pit is. I would go down there and blow out my candle and meditate, just trying to get a sense of what the whole thing was really about. I was very interested during my journey in trying to penetrate the mystery of Egypt. I was compelled to try and make some sense of what it was all about.

**ST:** Did you have any other experiences in Egypt you'd like to talk about?

**NS:** I recall Mountain Girl, Courtenay, and I went exploring one night. We wanted to see the Ship of the Sun. The Ship of the Sun is an ark, a wooden boat that was found in pieces buried along the pyramids. It was put together and encased in cement to make a museum. I don't know whether the museum is open to the public now but at that time it was definitely not open. There was still scaffolding around the building. We talked some guards into letting us look in. It was night time so they made us take off our shoes and go barefoot. We had to climb up the scaffolding along the side and on our tippy toes we could peer into the building, in the dark, and make out the shape of this exquisite boat, the Ship of the Sun, a magnificent relic that has laid for thousands of years without rotting or being disturbed. It was a beautiful thing.

We smoked a little hash with the guards and they started playing with us. They took us to a place where there was a broken off pillar of some sort. The guard boosted me up on it and motioned for me to face south. As soon as I turned and faced south toward the pyramid, my consciousness was completely opened. My perception had totally changed. The guard explained that this was the place where Pharaoh used to meditate and get his information. It was a frightening experience to feel that alteration of consciousness. It's like moving into a band of energy where suddenly your perception changes. The other thing the guards did was take us to the place where they dug up the Ship of the Sun. The pieces had been resting on huge stone slabs, which were sitting there. The guards began hitting on one and then another. It was like a great marimba and each piece had a different tone emanating from it as it was played. It was magical.

I remember that night Mountain Girl and I were sitting at the bottom of the pyramid and she was pointing out the different constellations to me. What a great place to be giving those kinds of lessons.

**ST:**   It sounds like you picked up on the energy of the pyramids.

**NS:**   There was just no way to miss it. The more awareness that you have, the more you have penetrated the veil by your own commitment and consciousness, the deeper and more rich that experience is because you're seeking to uncover the cognitive portion, and that's where the real interest is for me.

**ST:**   After the band returned from Egypt they played at Winterland.

JIM KOELLER

**From Egypt with love**

Winterland, October 21, 1978

**NS:** Oh, it was wonderful. Everybody came back influenced by Egypt. When those Winterland concerts took place, everybody dressed in Egyptian dress. Those were some of the most fun concerts that I remember because of the intensity of the energy. It's like whatever the music was lacking at the pyramids was twice made up for at home. The band should have called those shows their Egyptian shows and made an album of those concerts because they had all the inspiration and all the joy. The excitement of the journey was given out to the fans in those shows.

**ST:** The show on October 21, 1978 was just amazing.

**NS:** It was great. I really think the band managed to convey the whole feeling of Egypt through that series of concerts, and particularly that concert. They brought the magic of Egypt back and gave it to all the people that hadn't been there. The band was able to sustain the Egypt trip.

**ST:** Did you ever have any official capacity in the Dead organization?

**NS:** Not really an official capacity. I remember in early 1979 Jane Fonda invited the Grateful Dead to a meeting and asked them to do a benefit.

**ST:** Wasn't that the Rock for Life Benefit?

**NS:** Yes, it was at the Oakland County Coliseum. At that point the Dead decided that if they were going to do it, they might as well do it on a large scale. There were some problems and concerns and so I volunteered at that time to be the liaison between Bill Graham's organization and the Grateful Dead and ensure that the backstage and hospitality went smoothly. Of course, the Bill Graham organization was absolutely appalled that the band would allow me to take care of the backstage because I had no history of working. I had some meetings with them and heard about all the problems that they wanted changed. I devised a plan to make it work and went and got cooperation from everybody in the Grateful Dead so we would not have an unruly backstage scene. Everyone would be responsible for their guests and we would know in advance who was coming and what the limitations were. To balance that, we would have a real feast and make it a real party for ourselves because we would be doing such a large-scale benefit. So, within that, we really went out of our way to make it a fun thing to do as well.

When I came in I brought in the people that I wanted to do the work and displaced the other people that were doing the backstage hospitality. But what happened was it set a new standard. It changed things. I remember, by the end of the evening, I was called in by Bill Graham's people and given the Player of the Year Award for having really come through. I was never interested in a full-time job, nor was I interested in doing it for anything other than raising the quality of the experience for everybody.

I was then asked to participate and help with the Spartan Stadium event, which was a couple of months later in April 1979. I talked Bill Graham into letting me use his exquisite antique appliqued Egyptian tent for a special backstage place. The other thing I remember about that concert was that it was when the child-care scene was instituted. It was the Barsottis' idea and they asked me who could do it. We created a babysitting environment where all the kids could go. We had so many children in the backstage scene. That's when I thought of the Hog Farm and we invited them to start doing it. It has now become an institution at a Grateful Dead show. It's a safe place where parents can leave their kids and know they'll be taken care of, entertained, and nourished in every way. It's run by the Hog Farm who keeps a revolving staff there. Wavy Gravy is often there and different entertainers come in. It's a scene within a scene, which is really wonderful. I know when my kids were little we didn't have anything like that. It was very different and sometimes a strange place for kids to run around. The babysitting scene made a large difference in the quality of the concerts from that time on, especially for the family.

ST: Tell me about the Warfield run in 1980. Whose idea was it to toast the Grateful Dead?

NS: As far as I know, that was one of Bill Graham's gems. It was his way of saying thank you to the band and he did it in such a tasteful way. There was something about that run of shows that is different from all others. It came out in a lot of ways. During the first couple of nights, Bill would go around with a tape recorder. Every flaw he would find he would note it on his tape recorder. The next day it would be transcribed, and whatever criticisms he found would be changed by that next night. Because he had time to do this, by halfway through the run it was perfect. It was flawless, in terms of the production. It created the space to allow the music and all of us to get high, safely, in a good way. There became a closeness between the people producing the show and those of us that were involved with the family and the performance. There was interaction at a much closer level. My greatest fun during those shows was giving away whatever comp tickets were left.

The last night Bill Graham brought enough champagne for all 2,200 people in the audience and during the last set he discreetly managed to have it served. Everyone had a plastic champagne cup. He had it arranged so that at the end of each row was a bottle of champagne and the cups for that row. It was done while the music was happening during the last set. Everybody was told to be cool. When the band went offstage, he placed a table out in the middle of the stage, with a tablecloth, a bucket for a champagne bottle, the champagne, and enough glasses for the band. That's all. The band came out and there it was. Right? Well, it was a complete surprise. They didn't know anything. They really didn't. They got out there and they were trying to figure out what they were supposed to do, and so they thought maybe they were supposed to toast the audience. Meanwhile, while they had been out, everybody was hustling the glasses and getting their own champagne poured and ready.

ST: This was before the encore?

NS: This was between the last set and the encore. That's not much time. So the band gets out there and they're fumbling around trying to figure out what they're supposed to do with this prop. They pour the glasses and hand it to each other, and they lift their glasses to toast the audience. You know, it was sort of natural. Suddenly the lights went on. The audience all put out their hands and there were 2,200 people toasting them. It was just amazing. It was really brilliant. It was one of the sweetest expressions that Bill had ever come up with.

Rock also thought of a wonderful gesture and decided that he wanted to give something back to all the people that were involved in the production. We were living with Jerry at the time and he found a sketchbook of Jerry's cartoons. Rock picked out several of the best of these cartoons and, with Jerry's permission, had them copied and made enough copies to give out to the security people, the production people, the production assistants, the people who watched the doors, all the people who helped put that fifteen-day run together. Most of the last couple of nights Rock was down in the dressing room framing them. Jerry even signed them. So that's one of those really special times where everybody got a piece of it.

**ST:** I understand there were comedy routines.

**NS:** We were staying at a motel in the city. At the time I was filling in the spaces of what needed to be done. So here we have Franken and Davis of *Saturday Night Live*. This was in preparation for the simulcast for a Halloween happening in New York at Radio City. We were preparing the script and getting it together. We were using the Warfield gig to get the skits down so when we were doing it live in New York, it would be done right. The rehearsals were all in California. It started out that we were in a motel room in the City developing a script. Someone had an idea for Jerry's kids and we needed to find the poster kids. I got on the phone and put the word out and set up the interviews. I put out a call for sincere and dedicated Dead Heads that looked the part but were articulate and not too flaky. They came and interviewed with Garcia at the hotel. I brought them in, greeted them, and got them out. I ran that whole part of it. That's how we met Dennis McNally.

**ST:** The band's publicist?

**NS:** Yes, he came in and applied for the job. Before I would take anybody in to see Jerry, I would interview them. He told me who he was and that he had written Kerouac's biography. I took him in and introduced him to Jerry. I guess Jerry had read his book. I can't remember his words, they were really funny. But, basically, he gave him a lifetime pass, right off the top, based on the accomplishment of having written that book. But he wasn't really your perfect candidate for Jerry's kid because he wasn't that wacked-out looking. You've seen the poster — now he was perfect, right.

**ST:** Wasn't it Tumbleweed?

**NS:** Yes, it was Tumbleweed. Tumbleweed was perfect.

**ST:** He looks like Jerry's kid.

**NS:** He looks a perfect Jerry's kid. So Jerry's kid was a take-off on Jerry Lewis' MS kids. My part in this was staying up all night typing up the scripts and just doing whatever needed to be done. It was really a good time, putting this together, but it was a lot of hard work. Then the band went off to New Orleans, which I missed, on their way to New York. I went to New York and continued helping and was floored when I saw my name listed in the credits of the TV production. I had never expected the acknowledgment and only discovered it when I saw the video.

**ST:** So what was Radio City like?

**NS:** Radio City was good. First of all, we were recording it and our equipment didn't fit in. The first thing I remember about Radio City was having to carry our equipment in and having to go through a wall because the door wasn't big enough.

The shows were wonderful. The skits with Franken and Davis were just fabulous. The work that we put into creating the show was really terrific and everybody had a good time with it. There were some great skits. They were really funny.

The Halloween show was wild; right up there with one of those real special fun things that ever happened. In the Grateful Dead scene, those kind of special fun things happened frequently enough to keep it interesting. You know, as I talk to you and remember these things, it was exciting. I always felt very privileged to be able to participate and be a part of it. I enjoyed things like taking my kids to New York for *Saturday Night Live*.

I remember one time when we were staying at this posh hotel somewhere on the east side, somewhere in the East 50s and there were all these young prepubescent girls in the family. Two of them were mine and there were a few more of them at the hotel. I remember seeing Weir going jogging, trailed by a column of sweet pre-teenagers jogging to the park. Can you picture that? Bobby, ever mindful of his health and vigor, running through the streets of New York, followed by these little girls. There are vignettes, pictures like that in my mind, that I just love.

**ST:** It seems like the history of the band shows their motivating force was not financial gain — just something magical about the whole experience.

**NS:** It was, indeed, a very magical experience. That's why looking back at it, it was like being caught up in a wave. When I was a kid I used to swim in the ocean and I used to do a lot of body surfing. Sometimes you keep your head in front of a wave and if you move you get pummeled until you're sure you'll never draw another breath of air. Being within the Grateful Dead was kind of like that. You never really knew what was going to happen next. Consequently, you weren't really looking for it. You were just in the moment with it. It was just kind of unfolding and there didn't seem to be a lot of direction to it. It wasn't a great motivation for fame or a lot of money. It was the next step in front of us and how were we going to make it interesting and fun. It was always fraught with a certain level of intensity. I'd say, if anything, we were all intense with each other and it makes it hard to go out in the world, with that level of intensity, and find your niche because it's hard to be without it.

They've enhanced my life tremendously, but often from an adversarial position. You see, my personal struggles were for my own identity and following my spiritual calling within what was, ostensibly, a very spiritual trip. But it allowed for that.

ST: It seems that you were able to forge all of your positive experiences with the Grateful Dead into your life's work.

NS: Exactly. It is truly that. It is taking all of the positive visions and the positive forces of those experiences and allowing them in at a very deep level and then they are integrated and changed. Now, as it's coming out these years later, it is expressing that same positive vision at a whole other level of awareness and consciousness of reality. You see, for me, it's all in the Egyptian mysteries. That's my path of study and it's directly through that experience, or maybe the whole reason I was with the Grateful Dead, so that I could go to Egypt to make those initial connections, that I was awakened to what I could be. The synchronicities around my relationship with Egypt and the Grateful Dead are just wonderful.

Somehow the depth of my love for the Grateful Dead, and the music, and what it stood for, to me is expressed in who I am now and what I'm doing. How that energy was integrated and transformed by my being, in ways that I could never articulate and can't begin to understand, to be expressed in the spiritual work that I'm now doing. It's like the seed was germinated by the Grateful Dead and is now expressed in my life's work.

ST: Which is?

NS: Empowering people. Providing access to people to the knowledge, power, and wisdom that is inherent within their own being.

ST: Now there's a notion that when the Grateful Dead's music is in sync that you feel that you're being transported to a different place or different level of consciousness.

**NS:** I don't think so much that we're transported but that we expand to include much more of the possibilities and potential of life. After those experiences, one is no longer content with the ordinary or mundane. One wants to learn how to move through life with that level of consciousness, with that awareness that there is more. And my struggle was how to bring that into my ordinary reality. At concerts I would have these incredible, wonderful, intense experiences of knowing, of being at one with the whole of creation, of being awakened, of tickling areas of the universe that have never been explored by human consciousness. Now how do I bring that into my daily life? How do I keep from having to be like a yo-yo, struggling with the materialism and the conflicts of day-to-day actions ... and still maintain the memory of those experiences which are so far from the ordinary. As I grew older and matured, I realized that I couldn't bring the psychedelics into my day-to-day activities. I could only go to concerts when I could go to concerts, and although it was eternal at the moment, it was finite in the linear scheme of things. So it propelled me on a search that eventually took me away from itself. I had to leave the Grateful Dead in order to find what was the next level of expansion. I had to let go of the mother in order to find the nurturing within myself. That was a hard decision to make. When I did, the fruit yielded itself immediately — not that I could release all attachments to the Grateful Dead — no, in fact when I came to Eugene I hungered for the music and immediately set about to find a way to get them up here, and did, through the Field Trip.

But the seed of the Grateful Dead and all these experiences has brought forth the fruit of my life's work, rooted in the music and flowering in the Cauldron Teachings. It is still through returning to the music that I draw great strength and nourishment.

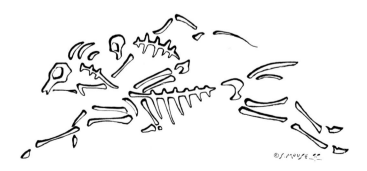

©J. MOUSE

# MICHAEL HINTON

Michael Hinton is a professional drummer and percussionist who has a Master in Music from Juilliard. In his youth Hinton took drum lessons from Mickey Hart before Hart joined the Grateful Dead. In addition to performing with a wide array of professional musicians, Hinton has joined his former drum teacher on stage to add his touch to the rhythm devils portion of the Dead's set. Hinton also participated in the making of the soundtrack to the film *Apocalypse Now* with Hart, Airto, Flora Purim and others.

**ST:** How did you meet Mickey Hart?

**MH:** Many years ago, when I was 12 years old, I was sort of teaching myself drums. A friend of mine asked me to check out a drum set that he was selling at Hart Music Center in San Carlos, California. Mickey and his father had a music store in San Carlos so I went down to the store to check out the drum set and Mickey was there and I started rapping with him. I told him I wanted to be a great drummer. So I started studying with him. Mickey put me on a very strict practice schedule. After five or six months, there was enough magic happening that he was very enthusiastic about teaching me. I was giving myself totally to studying with him so we started entering championships together. We entered the California State Championship. We would win everything we entered. I would enter junior division and he would enter senior division.

Mickey moved into my home after I knew him for about a year and a half. He had split up ownership of the music store with his dad.

**ST:** What year was this?

**MH:** This was 1966. So Mickey moved into my house and lived there for about a year. I used to have to hypnotize him because he was an insomniac. I was reading books on hypnosis at the time so I'd hypnotize him to go to sleep every night. I slept on the floor and he slept on the couch. I had a room with a drum set in it that I needed. He'd keep me awake practicing. This is true — he really tortured me — he was a great teacher.

One day we were at the Fillmore Auditorium when Count Basie was playing. We knew Sonny Payne, his drummer, and we were on stage when this guy came up to us and said, "If you're a friend of Sonny's, would you help me get on stage to meet him?" It was Bill Kreutzmann, who was a stranger to us at the time, so Bill met Sonny and hung out for a while. We got talking to Bill later and we played some drums and Bill was impressed and he started studying with Mickey. He started hanging out with us and we became friends. So Bill and Mickey became close and that was how the relationship developed between the Grateful Dead and Mickey.

Bill was a very solid rock drummer but he was intrigued with the technical end of drumming that Mickey and I were pursuing at the time.

**ST:** Did you jam with the Dead at that time?

**MH:** After Mickey joined the Dead in the fall of 1967, I jammed with them at some Fillmore concerts. I also played with Jorma Kaukonen and Jack Casady as a trio. We did a lot of experimental stuff on those Tuesday night Fillmore sessions.

**ST:** Did you play with the Airplane?

**MH:** I played with them for about eight months in 1968 when Spencer Dryden left the band, but I decided to pursue my own direction rather than join the band — much to Mickey's disappointment.

**ST:** Do you remember any specifics of shows when you jammed with the Dead?

**MH:** Mickey brought an influence into the band that was unique. For instance, Mickey is a drummer who wants to explore rhythmic ideas. He suggested possibilities about playing 7/8, and 11 and all those odd time signatures, and all the kinds of things that were drifting in from India and everywhere else. I remember one night we got together at the Fillmore, Bob Weir had a little thing, and Jerry had a little thing in seven,

and we all played on that. It was a full house of people and it was an incredible musical experience. Phil is such a great bass player. It's always fun to play with him.

There was a lot of rhythmic experimenting going on.

**ST:** Did you play on any of the Dead's albums?

**MH:** No, but I played on *Rolling Thunder*.

**ST:** Mickey has such diverse musical interests.

**MH:** Mickey has incredible energy, and the infusion of interests that he has brought to rock and roll is sort of like he was an ambassador to rock and roll — to help rock and roll expand its horizons. That's great, because it reaches many, many people.

BRIAN GOLD

Mickey has taken a kind of music that, before, was relegated to a limited role, and steered it into more diverse areas instead of that limited role.

**ST:** That's what is amazing about the Grateful Dead — they can integrate different motifs into their basic rock and roll music and have it be totally perfect and accepted by the audience. For instance, Egyptian music in the middle of a Grateful Dead jam, and it sounds like it belongs there.

**MH:** It sounds that way because everybody listens, and everybody is capable of responding to what they hear. That's the magic of the Grateful Dead. I've played with some very well-known jazz players that don't really listen or hear you, and these are people who are supposed to be great jazz players.

I've been on stage with the Grateful Dead in San Jose, for instance, in April of 1979, where Jerry played a triplet figure, and somebody took that and accented it. Pretty soon that triplet has developed, and the reason is because everybody listens to the subtle nuances.

**ST:** At Madison Square Garden in September of 1979 I noticed that you and Charles Perry joined Mickey and Billy on stage for the last night.

**MH:** Mickey is sort of the Papa Haydn of rock and roll. Haydn was called Papa Haydn because he looked after other musicians around him.

Mickey was bringing two generations of drummers on stage — his teacher, Charles Perry, and one of his former students, myself — which shows a real beautiful side of him. He laid back and let everybody else take it. That's the kind of sharing you don't find very often in people. It's a beautiful characteristic of Mickey that I want to bring out because it's rare in musicians to open the stage up.

**ST:** In fact, I noticed that he deferred to you and Charles entirely that night. He and Billy stopped playing altogether during the drum solo.

**MH:** I remember at one point that night I got the impulse to play "The Beast" and I picked up the sticks and walked over to it and before I even played a note, Mickey said "Go for it." I felt a sense of freedom to do whatever I felt at the time, which is great, because I was able to trust all my instincts. All of a sudden it was the Grateful Dead, Charles Perry from jazz, and me from Juilliard meeting there and making good music together. It was really beautiful.

Those nights at the Garden were something special. I went there on Tuesday just expecting to say hi to my old friend Mickey, and I got whisked up on the stage. The next thing you knew, we were playing, and then, by the third night, we were roaring together. That was a very high plane — really exciting, for all of us.

**ST:** Your solo was incredibly hot and creative. You really used "The Beast" to its utmost capacity.

**MH:** Thank you. When you get an instrument and it rings and it says music, and when you hear a sound that dictates to you and you're capable of meeting it, that's why you've practiced.

**ST:** How did you get involved with the making of the soundtrack for *Apocalypse Now*?

**MH:** Coppola went to a Dead concert and just flipped over the percussion and left a calling card for Mickey to come to his office. The way Mickey put it was that when Coppola presented him with the idea he had always wanted to do something like that. Mickey wanted to put together what he considered to be the gunfighters of percussion that would be capable of doing it and have the stamina to do it in the time that he had so he brought in a number of his friends to assist him. We recorded for 19 hours a day for 15 days and the last day we recorded for 24 hours. Coppola brought in a doctor to give us shots of Vitamin B to keep us from getting sick. It was very intense.

**ST:** Who worked on the sound?

**MH:** Mickey, Airto, Flora Purim, and me. Coppola left us alone with the film without any sound but helicopter noise, and talking. We began to watch the movie, immerse ourselves in it, and began to deal with the movie on its own level.

**ST:** The soundtrack is just unbelievable. How did you translate the story of the movie into music?

**MH:** We had the right instruments. Coppola sensed that before he ever asked us to do it. He tried the Hollywood string orchestras and various other typical approaches that did not work for the movie. I think it left him at the only logical place which was percussionists and real percussion instruments. Percussion can get into the psychology, the gut-level feelings, and the mind bendings of that movie, like that journey up the river, because there are sounds which illustrate psychological states in music, like fear.

**ST:** What were the different instruments you used?

**MH:** First of all we had a tubealong, which is a tuned steel instrument with 32 notes to the octave, made from steel and aluminum bars. 32 notes to the octave means that you can play notes that are so close together, like quarter tones, and gamelon scales, and things like that. We found scales that were pleasing and we found effects that were pleasing. We had a whole set of hollowed-out logs and a whole set of different-sized gongs.

We had Saul Goodman timpani, which is the timpani used in the New York Philharmonic. That made a big difference because those timpani are very special. We had Egyptian guitars, tamborellis, stuff in cans, a million different things like brake drums and all kinds of chimes made from brass and glass. We had little things that looked like Muslim architecture, pots with turbans that you hit, that are brass with points on each end and when you hit it, it spins, and the spinning causes a whirring sound. We had a thing that you spin that sounds like a helicopter and a tuned instrument like a bar with two very very low tones, close together, that you play like a fine electric Koto. We had Taiko drums from Japan, and we had a glass harp made from wine glasses that we collected and framed inside of wood resonating boxes. We had conga drums, "The Beast," roto drums, octagons, cricket calls, bird whistles, and baskets with sea shells in them and Brazilian instruments. Of course Airto brought up all of his stuff, all kinds of shakers and beans and things that you blow into.

Here we have a recording studio with the finest instruments in the whole world, and we're sending our guys out to rummage for tin cans. I got Ramrod at one point to get me a piece of pipe. I told Ramrod I wanted a pipe with holes in it at certain places and I wanted it a certain length. He brought me into a room with steel and aluminum pipes and we picked out the pipe and he drilled it to where it sounded right and we used it. What we had to do if we were ever to be successful was develop a whole repertoire of sounds, which meant giving up all of our preconceived ideas at times.

After we recorded the stuff we did in the studio, we brought it outdoors, put speakers around in this amphitheater, and then played with the speakers resonating in the amphitheater so we got a really natural outdoor sound. That was one of the things that Mickey came up with that I really liked.

ST:   Did any of the Dead other than Mickey get involved?

**MH:** Bill got involved and did some playing on the African talking drum. Phil Lesh did some bass and timpani parts. Phil is a wonderful bass player. When he plays, you listen, and you react. He can come in on anything that you are doing and play circles around it and really make you dance.

**ST:** From your perspective as a professional musician, how would you describe Grateful Dead music?

**MH:** The Grateful Dead are capable of speaking more dialects of music than just one. That's the Grateful Dead's magic. If art educates, then the Grateful Dead, through their genius, are teaching you something about music. Like the motto on Mickey's t-shirt said: GOD IS SOUND.

SANDY TROY

Phil Lesh

JAY BLAKESBERG

## BRENT MYDLAND

Brent Mydland joined the Grateful Dead as their keyboardist in April 1979 replacing Keith and Donna Godchaux. Mydland's versatility as a keyboardist and his vocal harmonies injected new life into the band. Mydland's musical style and songwriting abilities helped make the Dead albums *Go to Heaven*, *In the Dark*, and *Built to Last* more accessible to the mainstream audience.

**ST:** How long have you been playing music?

**BM:** I started playing piano when I was about six or seven, so I've been playing now for about twenty years. I had classical training when I was a youngster and basically played classical music for seven or eight years.

**ST:** What type of music did you expand into after classical?

**BM:** Rock and roll. I revolted. At first, I just tinkered around by myself, making up tunes. My first band was in high school. I remember we had a tone-deaf bass player and a drummer that knew two beats—one that was fast and one that was slow.

**ST:** When you were starting out, who were your major influences as far as your style of playing the keyboards is concerned?

**BM:** One of my favorites, when I began playing rock and roll, was Pigpen. I also liked Jimmy Smith and the Doors' Ray Manzarek. Later I got into Herbie Hancock and Chick Corea.

**ST:** When did you decide to go into music professionally?

**BM:** I don't know if it was ever my goal or not. I just kind of fell into it. I never really thought about doing anything else. I just ended up in a band that ended up making money.

**ST:** What would you consider your first step as a professional in the music business?

**BM:** That's kind of hard to say. I started out in the early '70s playing high schools, recreation centers, and parties, like everyone else, I guess. Later, I hit the club circuit, but I never really got into it. In 1975, I went down to L.A. and formed a band called Silver. We recorded an album on Arista Records that was released in 1976. I also did some session work before that, but that was my first album.

**ST:** What did you do after that?

**BM:** Bob Weir was looking for a band to do a tour to back up his album, *Heaven Help the Fool*, which he had already cut. I met Bob through John Mauceri, a drummer who I played with when I was living in L.A. John told Bob that he knew a keyboard player who also sang, which is what Bob was looking for. The funny thing was that Bob lives in the Bay Area, yet I ended up meeting Bob in L.A. Anyway, I went on a six-week East Coast tour with the Bob Weir Band. We also did a few short tours on the West Coast.

**ST:** When did you get the call to join the Dead?

**BM:** Sometime in February 1979. Bob gave me a call and asked me if I was interested.

**ST:** Did you have to audition?

**BM:** I guess it was pretty much of an audition. I don't think they tried anyone else out, but they did want to hear me. Some of the band had heard me before with Bob's band. I went to their studio and played with them, and apparently they liked the way I played.

**ST:** Your style of playing fits into the band perfectly, like you've been playing with the Dead for years.

**BM:** It's pretty much natural, being that I grew up in the Bay Area. I don't think I would have been considered a Dead Head, but I liked the Dead. Even though I didn't go to all their concerts, I was familiar with a lot of the music they played. I think we have the same influence, being from the same general area — we phrase vocal licks the same.

**ST:** Do you find it difficult to play the Dead's improvisational style of music?

**BM:** No, on the contrary, I enjoy it. I just flow with it. Improvisation is the type of music I like playing the most. It's what keeps the spark in the music.

**ST:** It's what keeps the fans interested too.

**BM:** It's what keeps it fun for everyone concerned, including the band.

**ST:** How do you see your role in the band with respect to the interplay of your keyboards and the other instruments?

**BM:** I see it as both a textural instrument and a lead instrument. I can go between the two—there's room for both. I try to think of the dynamics of the music as well as melody, harmony, and all the textures. I think the whole band is really dynamic. All the members of the band listen to each other and work off of each other. No one person dominates the music.

**ST:** Garcia's sense of rhythm and melody, as well as Weir's penchant for odd chord inversions and ability to play beautiful instrumental harmonies, must be a real inspiration to you.

**BM:** It gives me the opportunity to be creative. I listen to different sections of the band and try to complement different people at different times, which makes things interesting, in that it can be different and keeps things flowing.

It's also nice to have the two drummers in the group. In a lot of groups with two drummers, they're just playing the same thing. But in this band, one drummer is usually on fills while the other is doing the basic track. I can watch them and it gives me something to go by.

**ST:** Phil Lesh really gets into the dynamics of the bass. He uses it as a lead and rhythm guitar as well as a bass guitar. Phil lays out bass tones that open up and have dimension. You can almost visualize those incredible 10Hz notes coming from his bass and expanding out into the room. How does this affect you?

**BM:** Sometimes it plays with my head—that's what it does. Phil doesn't just play the standard bass licks and roots. He's all over the instrument. You name it and he'll put it in there.

ANDREW SOPCZYK

**ST:** Does working in the studio interfere at all with the mental state you need to be in when you are out on the road, performing live?

**BM:** When we are in the studio, we're working on one song at a time, trying to get it just right. When we're out on the road performing live, we're going through the list of tunes we play and it gets tighter the more you keep at it. Being in the studio, and going over just one tune, we are not doing the other tunes in our repertoire. It takes a couple of days of being on the road to get into the groove.

**ST:** Over the years, the Grateful Dead organization seems to have evolved into something more than a business.

**BM:** It is something more. It's not just a business — it's one big family. Everybody in the organization cares about each other. The Grateful Dead have made music fun again for me. It got to a point a few years ago when I felt music was more business than anything. Now it's fun to play again. The Grateful Dead have been able to withstand the pressures of the business.

**ST:** The Dead seem to be very concerned about their fans. The band is known for its extensive concert tours and also for the legions of loyal Dead Heads who follow the Dead around wherever they play.

**BM:** If it wasn't for all those people out there, we wouldn't be playing. Thank God they're out there and they like our music. I know everyone in the band, myself included, likes playing on the road more than doing anything else.

**ST:** It's been said that certain forms of music have been known to induce an alpha state in people. Part of the audience's interest in the Grateful Dead may stem from a desire to achieve such a state of consciousness.

**BM:** I think that's right. When music gets into improvisation, it's totally what you feel at the time, and everybody else is influencing you. What everybody else is playing influences you. How the audience is responding influences you. The whole thing put together is magic!

The Author & Brent Backstage
at Madison Square Garden,
September 1979

## ALEC LEVY

In the early '70s Alec Levy was Student Union Board Chairman at Suffolk Community College and in that capacity produced concerts. While booking concerts he met and became friends with Rock Scully. Upon moving to California Levy got a job booking travel arrangements for the Grateful Dead when the Dead's own travel agency Fly By Night Travel disbanded.

**ST:** Al, could you give me some background information about how you got involved in the music business?

**AL:** I was the Student Union Board Chairman at Suffolk Community College in New York and as part of that job you had to produce concerts. The students paid an activity fee. You weren't supposed to make any money because money left over would go back to the Board of Trustees. I was making money charging $2.00 a ticket so that's when I left school and did it on my own for five years or so.

**ST:** What concerts did you produce?

**AL:** Miles Davis, Eric Clapton and Derek and the Dominoes, McKenzie Spring, Jonathan Edwards, Dave Von Ronk. I also managed two clubs — one in the Hamptons and one in Stony Brook in New York.

**ST:** What clubs?

**AL:** The Scorpio Room — it was a folk club that was open until four in the morning, sometimes six. We stopped serving booze at two.

The other club was the Barbary Coast in the Hamptons, which was a summer club.

**ST:** How did you get involved with the Grateful Dead organization?

**AL:** I met Rock Scully. The first time the New Riders played without the Dead was part of a music festival in Virginia, at William and Mary College, called the Virginia County Music Festival around 1972. I helped promote it with two other promoters.

Then, when I moved to California, I became a travel agent in Marin County for a company that did the travel for a lot of rock bands — the Dead, Starship, Pablo Cruise, Bobby Weir, Joan Baez, and the Doobie Brothers.

Randy Sarti, who was my boss, had been doing the Dead for years. There's a funny story of why the Dead picked Randy — he was working at a different travel agency in Marin before he opened his own. The Dead had their own travel agency called Fly By Night Travel, which they disbanded. They were looking for a new agent at the agency where Randy worked, and he was the only one there with a mustache so they chose him. It was a real feather in his cap because the Dead were some account — a lot of trips, $10,000 bar bills.

He not only did the trips, he did all the trucks, the rental cars, all the hotel rooms, and all the air fares. Randy was so good as a travel agent that he would prepare a book for every tour they went on, which everybody in the band got, including the roadies and the truck drivers, which had everything laid out in it day by day—load in, load out, who's gonna go where, what hotels they're gonna stay at, etc.

He made up a book which was sent to the printer and distributed to them. He was really professional. I've never seen any other agency do that.

ST:   What tours did you work on?

AL:   I worked on a bunch of them. I was in charge of booking the family members, Dead Heads, Hells Angels, and friends.

The first phone call I got was from Danny Rifkin, who was one of the managers of the Grateful Dead. He called me and asked me to do him a favor. He wanted it to be clear that since I was privy to all the inside information about the band that I should keep it on the QT. That was the hardest part of my job, not being able to tell any of my friends what I knew. It made sense though. I remember there was one girl, whose name was May, who had a thing for Bob Weir and she kept hassling him. When I went to Alaska with the Dead, we were on the flight back and she was on the same flight. This girl, May, snuck up to first class where the band was sitting and she sat right down next to them. The next thing I knew, she was covered in booze. Someone had poured their drink on her head. All this booze is dripping off of her head. The stewardess came up and asked who did it. May didn't want to get anyone in trouble so she wouldn't say—she said it was their manager Scully who, of course, had nothing to do with it, since he was sitting all the way in the back of the plane in coach.

ST:   This was when the Dead played Anchorage, Alaska, in June 1980?

AL:   Yeah. I flew up with the band and the flight to Alaska was pretty wild. As I recall, it was a champagne flight. The airline was giving out complimentary champagne. The plane was full of Dead Heads and everybody got pretty toasted. As I recall, everybody stayed at the Hilton Hotel.

ST:   How were the shows?

AL:   The whole experience was pretty wild. You wouldn't believe it. The sun didn't set the whole time we were there. The shows were during the summer solstice. They were at

West High School in Anchorage. I remember I was in the bar drinking with Jerry and he said the band thought the sound was weird — it kept bouncing off the walls because the auditorium was so small. The soundman, Healy, worked on the sound for three days.

The only other wilder thing I ever did with the band was when we did the World Music Festival in Jamaica. That was unbelievable. I chartered the whole thing.

**ST:** That was in November of 1982?

**AL:** Barry Fey, the promoter from Colorado, did it with the President of Jamaica. They got together and put on a three-day World Music Festival.

**ST:** What bands were there?

**AL:** The Dead, of course. Bob Weir's band was there — Kingfish, also the Clash, the Squeeze, the Melody Makers, Judy Mowatt, and others.

**ST:** Was there a chartered flight from San Francisco?

**AL:** All the major cites in the U.S. had chartered flights. Each city had one travel agent. I was handling the Bay Area. I had 199 people on the plane. We had a Dead Head charter called Dead Air that was the wildest thing. Dead Heads were dancing in the aisle to Dead music. There were 99 people on this plane that I was directly responsible for — 99 concert-goers who paid $700.00 each. This included concert tickets for three days and hotel accommodations at Runaway Bay. I had to bus them to the concert which was at the Bob Marley Memorial in Montego Bay, fifty miles away.

But the real kicker was that these people weren't just Dead Heads, who are mellow and peaceful; there were also Clash Heads and Rasta Heads — a real diverse group of people whom I was babysitting as part of the charter.

And there were members of the Dead office staff, as well as friends of the band. Wavy Gravy was on the plane, Eileen Law, Sue Stephens, Freddie Herrera, the guy who runs the Keystones, Summer, the lady who makes Grateful Dead quilts, and Hell's Angels.

I had this wild plane. I had all the Dead Heads, a bunch of Hell's Angels, Clash Heads, and every freak known to music on my plane and everybody had their own ghetto blaster!

The Dead Heads ran the plane. Everybody was blowing weed like crazy. I had to make the announcements over the P.A. on the plane to tell people not to smoke reefers on the

BRIAN GOLD

**Wavy Gravy**

plane. While I'm doing this, people are coming up to me and sticking joints in my mouth.

This was a real zoo plane.

Not only that, dig this, we picked up part of the football team from Denver — all the guys with four-foot necks who are going to work security for Feyline Productions at the concert.

How do you think they related to the Dead Heads, Clash Heads, weed, and ghetto blasters — these football players are all sitting in a group flipping out. The music is blaring — all different kinds, Dead music, the Clash, reggae, and the plane is like a cloud of smoke.

**ST:** What was the scene like in Jamaica?

**AL:** As soon as you get off the plane the Jamaicans were trying to sell you weed.

I'm the tour coordinator trying to keep it all together and I was responsible for all these people getting to the concert, etc.

The concert in Jamaica went from 8:00 at night to 7:00 in the morning. The Dead came on at 4:00 in the morning.

**ST:** How were the other acts?

**AL:** The shows were good, but long and disorganized.

**ST:** How did the band like it?

**AL:** They stayed in Montego Bay at the Holiday Inn International and they had a good time. They also had the best backstage scene of any band at the shows. The shows were right by the water and there was a boat just offshore with an indoor cabin that the band used as their backstage. Out of all the bands there, the Dead had the most elite place — they had their own boat to hang out in.

**ST:** How was the flight back?

**AL:** It was wilder than the flight there!

**ST:** What kind of interaction have you had with Jerry Garcia?

**AL:** Well, when I moved out to California, I happened to meet Maria Maldaur and we became friends. Her old man at the time was John Kahn, who plays bass guitar in the Jerry Garcia Band, and that's how I became friends with Jerry.

Jerry's a real nice guy. The first time I met Jerry he said to me, "I've been seeing you around for years at shows; you don't pay anything to get into the shows, do you?" Maybe he thought I knew somebody or whatever, and I said: "What do you think, they let me in for free?" I haven't had to pay for another show since! Jerry's one of the most well-read persons I've ever met but what he loves most is music. I've been backstage on many occasions when everybody's sitting around socializing and relaxing, and Jerry will be sitting off to the side with a small Peavey amp and his guitar, practicing runs and warming up for the show.

When the Dead played the Rainbow in London in 1981 I was there. I was checking into the hotel and these two guys came up to me from behind and put their arms around me to say hello and it was Jerry and Rock and we hung out together.

We all stayed at the same hotel in London. It was wild.

ST:   What hotel?

AL:   The Kensington Palace by Hyde Park, there was a guy with a top hat at the door. In England the pubs close early, 11:00-11:30, but in the hotel they kept the pub open until 1:30 for the band so we could party. Phil Lesh was drinking Heinekens at the time. He would take a bottle, and when he was finished, he would put the empty bottle in his pocket. I remember he kept dropping bottles out of his pocket on to the floor. It was pretty funny.

ST:   Do you have any favorite places to see the Dead play?

AL:   The Oregon Country Faire in Veneta is my favorite place of all. It's outdoors, there's no police, no security, and just mellow people doing a mellow job in real grasslands. Kesey's there and it's a real good time.

I also like the Warfield in San Francisco. I went to all fifteen shows they played in 1980. It was quite a run of shows. The Warfield is a great place to see the Dead. The band did acoustic sets every night before the electric sets. They played 97 different songs in those fifteen nights, which I thought was pretty amazing. The backstage scene was loose. Franken and Davis were there and did comedy routines. They did a takeoff on Jerry Lewis — Jerry's kids. My friend Tumbleweed was Jerry's kid.

They showed Steve Parish running around with a buzz saw that reminded me of the closing of Winterland on New Year's 1978 — when Belushi was there. It was phenomenal. Backstage at Winterland, Belushi was a maniac, doing cartwheels in the hallways.

Red Rocks is pretty cool too. It always rains there. I was

sitting on stage with my wife, Annie, right behind the drummers the first night—I'm talking I could've grabbed the sticks out of Mickey's hands. The greatest drums I had ever seen. We were slightly inebriated, to say the least, and they played the drum solo so loud it echoed off the mountains.

The second night we're in the same spot, we're having a great time and it starts to pour, but the concessions are ready for it—they sell these orange ponchos for $5.00. If you're on the stage you watch the place slowly turn orange all around you. It goes from tie-dyes and t-shirts to pure orange and it's strange.

New York's an electric place to see the band. The Dead love New York. When they play Madison Square Garden they play louder and more intense. The band tells the soundman to turn it up.

**ST:** I've heard band members say they feel New York made them.

**AL:** The Dead became a cult in New York. The Dead were leaders; they personified the West Coast '60s psychedelic movement.

**ST:** The Dead took the East Coast by storm playing places like the Fillmore East and college campuses.

**AL:** The Dead played at Stony Brook, which is part of the State University of New York. In 1970 they played four shows there on Halloween weekend.

The concerts at Stony Brook were unbelievable. They turned the house. Each night there was an 8 o'clock and 11 o'clock show. After the first show you're supposed to make everyone leave and bring in the new crowd, except the Dead let everyone stay.

When the Dead came to New York they weren't thinking in terms of making money. Don't forget I was promoting concerts back then, and it was known within the industry that the Dead didn't care about making money; money wasn't important to them. They had very existential views on life.

**ST:** What's the band's current philosophy?

**AL:** I've heard a family member say it better than I could— "There's the right way, the wrong way, and the Grateful Dead way."

COURTESY OF SANDY TROY

All Hallow's Eve, October 31, 1970, Stony Brook, N.Y.

## DICK LATVALA

Dick Latvala is the Grateful Dead tape archivist. Latvala grew up in the San Francisco Bay Area and participated in LSD experiments in 1965 as part of a research project. One of the original Dead Heads, he has been "on the bus" since first seeing the Dead at the Trips Festival in January 1966. Latvala had seen hundreds of shows prior to being employed by the Dead in 1985.

ST: I understand that you work for the Grateful Dead.

DL: Yes, I'm in charge of the tapes in the vault, cataloging and organizing them, and making some sense out of it all.

ST: You're the archivist.

DL: I guess you can call me that. I do whatever is necessary but that's what I should be doing.

ST: How did you get involved with the Grateful Dead scene?

DL: In 1964 I heard Alpert and Leary talk about LSD research so I took LSD in 1965 as part of a research project in Menlo Park. I started going to Grateful Dead concerts in 1966. The first one I went to was the Trips Festival at Longshoremen's Hall in January 1966. The Grateful Dead played and some other groups that I can't remember. I remember Bill Graham running around with his clipboard and Kesey and the Pranksters doing some audio-visual things all over the place.

ST: LSD was still legal at that time.

DL: Yes. It really turned me around and I was enamored when I saw that scene at the Trips Festival. I realized I was supposed to be at that kind of thing and not at college where I was trying to perform in a way that pleased my parents. Although I was a good student and even graduated with a degree, I knew the thrill of music is what made sense to me. I had no idea where it would lead to but I just knew that it was what I wanted to do and that's what I've been doing ever since that time. In 1966 I went to more shows than any year.

LSD was something that turned me around. I was reformulating my basic foundations of how to think abstractly. That really put a crinkle in my system. What the LSD represented was a way of approaching the universe, intellectually or philosophically. But also in music, what these groups were playing was different than what was going on before that.

ST: Non-linear?

DL: Yes. It wasn't following or copying a tradition particularly. It was just different. That's why they call it psychedelic music.

The first music I ever thought was cool was gospel music. In 1959 I started going to the Oakland Auditorium to see gospel concerts. Every couple of months they would have James Leland, The Soul Stirrers, Mighty House of Joy, and a bunch of other famous gospel groups. There were mostly black people at the concert and they would be dressed in their Sunday best and there would be ushers all around the building. When the music got going people would have epileptic-type reactions to the music, which had something to do with God of course, and I remember seeing this one guy run from the back of the auditorium, right down the aisle, and dive head first on to the stage.

I was part of the 1% of the white people in the building. What came to me from that situation is that music should have an emotional effect on you instead of the effect white people's music had, like *Hit Parade* with Dean Martin, Perry Como, and Patti Page. I didn't like the God part particularly, but the basic thing is that it was music that hit you. Then came the psychedelic thing. The Grateful Dead and all these other groups came along after acid and in that same time frame. It was like the first thing I heard and it knocked me out emotionally.

ST:  Did you go to any of the free concerts the Dead played at?
DL:  I remember the day LSD was made illegal there was some kind of celebration in the Panhandle, October 6, 1966.

ST:  That was the Love Pageant Rally.
DL:  I remember the Dead played on a flatbed truck and that Kesey's psychedelic bus was there.

ST:  Did you go to the Fillmore Auditorium?
DL:  I remember the Mothers of Invention were at the Fillmore with Lenny Bruce in July 1966. The Fillmore was a tiny place and in the hallway where you went upstairs, there was this little bay window with a bench in it. At the break I sat down there just to get a breather. Lenny Bruce came up and sat down next to me and Allen Ginsberg sat on the other side. Those two got into an argument while I'm sitting there right in the middle of them. It was a trip!

Most of the shows I went to were in 1966 and 1967. This was a really formative period for the music. No one knew where it was going to lead. That was particularly exciting for hippies or people into LSD. I would go ripped on acid. I realized that I liked to take acid and see the Grateful Dead. But it didn't matter if you took acid because the Grateful Dead were like an acid trip.

I remember by 1968 the Grateful Dead certainly was "it" for me. I went to shows that really made me feel emotions like gospel music does for black people. There was an emotional element to it.

**ST:** How many Dead shows do you think you have been to over the years?

**DL:** In 1966 I went to lots more shows than any other year. I've probably been to a total of 300 but that's difficult to estimate. I just know that I went to enough to know that I'm hooked. There's no hope any more, mom!

**ST:** Now you were talking about how exciting it was, and you alluded to the notion that this music was breaking new ground — improvisational music linking consciousness to feelings.

**DL:** It reflected a new way of relating to the universe. My mind was wanting something new. The Eisenhower years bored a lot of people. I wanted something that would connect intellectual knowledge with emotional knowledge. Music was a reflection of the appetite to want to explore or discover something different.

What was exciting about psychedelic music was the jamming and improvisation. The groups weren't just sticking to the three- or four-minute song. In fact at the April '69 show at the Avalon, someone pulled the plug on the electronics during "Viola Lee Blues" at the end of the show but the microphones were still working so they did an a capella ending to it. That type of expansion beyond the limitations of normal records is what I thought psychedelic music was about.

**ST:** Did you go to the Monterey Pop Festival in 1967?

**DL:** It was great. Each night six or seven groups played and it was intense. A lot of it was shocking. For instance, seeing the Who smashing their guitars, and Hendrix lighting his guitar on fire. I was camping on the football field with a bunch of other concert-goers who needed a place to crash. The football field belonged to the college next to the festival site. One night a flatbed truck was set up on the football field for all the people camping there and Eric Burdon and the Animals played, and some other groups. It was wild. Everybody was stoned on acid.

**ST:** How did the Dead play?

**DL:** Compared to all the incredible things that went down they didn't really stand out as anything special.

**ST:** Did you go to the Carousel ballroom?

**DL:** Yes. The Airplane, the Dead, and Quicksilver were involved and they promoted shows at the Carousel ballroom for about three or four months. Graham took it over and renamed it the Fillmore West.

**ST:** You were quoted in *DeadBase* as saying that the Dead show from the Fillmore West on March 1, 1969 was the best show you ever witnessed. What was it about that show that was so great?

**DL:** When I started collecting tapes, I was trying to find things that really blew my mind. This 3/1/69 show was one of the first I found that really reminded me of everything that was going on. What killed me was when I listened to it on tape and realized that I had been there. After hearing it on tape I realized it was some of the greatest music I had ever heard. I'm totally convinced of it. It's absolute excitement from beginning to end. The first set is about 44 and a half minutes straight through. Graham comes out and says something like the American version of the Japanese movie, *The Magnificent Seven*, the Grateful Dead. He even introduces them again in the second set opening with some other cute introduction. The show opens with "That's It for the Other One" when they also did "New Potato Caboose." Phil gets into this bass solo in it. It was really unique. At the end of "That's It for the Other One" the music builds up to a crescendo but instead of hitting that final chord they drop down into "Doing That Rag" and it sounds great. Then "Cosmic Charlie" starts off fast and furious and ends the set. After the break, the second set continues with "Dupree's Diamond Blues" into "Mountains of the Moon," then an incredible "Dark Star" into "St. Stephen" into "The Eleven" into "Lovelight" and a mindblowing encore of "Hey Jude." The thing that I discovered while listening to the 1969 tapes in the archives is that they used to start acoustically and do "Mountains of the Moon," as an opening tune, into an acoustic version of "Dupree's Diamond Blues" and near the end of "Dupree's" they would subtly switch to electric and go into "Dark Star." That was common for shows during that period of time.

**ST:** Wasn't *Live Dead* recorded at that run of shows at the Fillmore West at the end of February 1969?

**DL:** I think that *Live Dead* is from February 27, 1969 which was the first show of the run. Those four shows were as good as it gets!

**ST:** Can you describe the evolution of Grateful Dead music through the years?

**DL:** Starting in 1965 and through 1966 the Dead had a sound that was a cross between a twangy garage band and an electric blues band with Pigpen doing a lot of the vocals. In 1966 Pigpen sang more of the tunes than he did later on. For instance in 1971 if he did five songs it was a lot. Back in 1966 that was normal. The vocalization rapping that Pigpen got into was developed over a period of time from the early days. A tune like "Midnight Hour" was a long tune that ended the show and is a good early example of Pigpen's rapping style of singing. "Lovelight" is another example of that style of singing. Pigpen started doing "Lovelight" in 1967. By 1967 the band started expanding their repertoire and their musical style became more improvisational. Songs like "Alligator" into "Caution" and "Lovelight" were extravagant explorations and a little bit bent. By 1968 the sound really crystallized into psychedelic music. With the addition of Mickey Hart into the band a whole new rhythmic dimension was added that was insane. It was really experimental jamming that was very exciting. In 1969 the band reached its peak in terms of that style of experimental music with Constanten in the band. "Alligator" into "Caution" was a good vehicle for improvisation and could be extended into an awesome piece of music. A good example is the one from February 28, 1969. The "Alligator" is really extended and was incredible. Starting in 1970 the band played a more limited version of "Alligator."

With the departure of TC in early 1970 the band changed from that wildly experimental phase. They simplified somewhat and were performing the songs from *Workingman's Dead* and *American Beauty*. They continued in the psychedelic style of the '60s but some of the more improvisational pieces were condensed somewhat, but not all of them by any means. While the style of the music may have changed their inspirational essence remained the same. There were still some insane "Dark Star"s and wild "Lovelight"s. People consider February 13 and 14, 1970 to be some of the best music the Dead ever performed. Also the run of shows at the Capitol Theatre in Portchester in November of 1970 has some outrageous jamming. With the departure of Mickey Hart in February of 1971 the band had to simplify some more of the arrangements but by that time the band had a large amount of original songs, which reflected Robert Hunter's proliferation as a songwriter.

**ST:** Many of the songs from *Workingman's Dead* and *American Beauty* were not vehicles for improvisational jamming.

**DL:** After the band had been going off into outer space for so many years there was nowhere left to go. After a period of time of going to the outer reaches there was a need to crystallize things in a way that the public at large could relate to. After Constanten and Mickey left things changed. In September of 1971 Keith Godchaux joined the band and by the fall of 1971 Pigpen was already suffering from being ill and his influence on the band was decreasing. In fact the Europe '72 tour was Pigpen's last tour. With the addition of Donna Godchaux the band was definitely in a state of transition. By the end of 1972 with Pigpen no longer performing the music changed. The band introduced that new sound system that evolved into the "wall of sound." Songs like "Eyes of the World" and "Playing in the Band" became the vehicles for extensive jamming, along with "Dark Star." It seemed like the band was getting jazzier at times. In fact in the fall of 1973 the band played with a horn section at several shows. Listen to the "Dark Star" from Keil Auditorium on October 30, 1973. It has a real uptempo jazzy attack as opposed to an introspective approach that "Dark Star"s had in 1969 or 1970. Take a listen to the "Dark Star" from Miami on June 23, 1974. It is an instrumental with a real jazzy feel to it. "Eyes of the World" was also a song that lent itself to a jazzy sound. With the "wall of sound" the band had the desire to make the sound blow away the audience in terms of quality and the band went for that smooth sound. By 1974 the sound system got so big that the whole scene had to break up for a while. During the break the Dead worked out the *Blues for Allah* material which was more complicated. For instance the "Help on the Way" into "Slipknot" into "Franklins Tower" medley is a more involved arrangement. Look at the SNACK Benefit. The "Blues for Allah" jam from that show is different from anything else they have ever done. By 1976 the Dead were in the midst of the Keith and Donna era. The band brought back some of the classic songs from the '60s like "St. Stephen" and "Cosmic Charlie," which is always exciting. It took a while for the band to get going but there are some real good shows from 1976. The Orpheum run in July had some excellent shows, and the Shrine shows in October are outstanding. The New Year's show is very good and by 1977 the band was really cooking. The band introduced the songs "Terrapin" and "Estimated Prophet" in San Bernardino, and got the year off to a great start. Then they debuted "Fire on the Mountain" at Winterland in March. At this point in time the band was playing with inspiration and there were many excellent shows during the remainder of the year. In 1978 the band started having problems with Keith and Donna and the general consensus among Dead Heads is that '78 was basically a low point, though there were some very good moments that year. The band went to Egypt and fulfilled one of their dreams. The shows at Winterland when they returned were really inspired, and people consider October 21, 1978, one of the best shows ever. The closing of Winterland on December 31, 1978 was also one of the legendary shows. The show at Oakland Coliseum on February 17, 1979 was the end of an era since it was Keith and Donna's last show with the Dead. It started the new era with Brent Mydland. When Brent joined the band it was a positive influence. He brought new energy into the music. The band has played some incredible shows with Brent. May 6, 1981 at Nassau is one of my favorite shows, and there are lots of other good shows. Brent is a good song-

GREG GAAR

Winterland, March 1977

writer and has contributed his songs to the repertoire. The albums *Go to Heaven*, *In the Dark*, and the new album *Built to Last* seem to appeal to the mainstream more. *In the Dark* went platinum and was in the top ten and I felt really good about that because I had done a lot of work on that album. In fact I'm proud to say I received a platinum album for my efforts, which was a total surprise in that I never expected it. The new album *Built to Last* is well produced and I think it is their best one yet. My favorite tunes are "Blow Away" and "Foolish Heart."

**ST:** What was it like when the Dead started playing with Dylan?

**DL:** I was working at the studio on Front Street in January 1987 when I heard that Dylan would be coming to rehearse with the band for two days to see if the collaboration would work out. I was in the studio working when Dylan showed up and it looked to me like they were having a good time rehearsing. About a month later Dylan phoned Jerry up and said it's a go, let's do it. That resulted in a 21-day rehearsal schedule in May. Dylan showed up for the rehearsals with his manager Elliot Roberts. The Dead and Dylan ran over a lot of songs, some of which didn't get played on the tour. They rehearsed so many songs out of left field that there were seven books of songs that were prepared for them by Annette at the Dead office. I think there were eighty or so songs that they rehearsed. There were a lot of tunes that weren't even Dylan tunes. They rehearsed some Dead tunes, in fact. It was great!

Part of my job aside from being the archivist is to serve as a go-fer and do whatever is needed for the band when they are rehearsing or are working in the studio on an album. On this occasion I was getting lunches and dinner for the guys. I asked Elliot Roberts if I should get anything for Dylan and he says, "Do whatever's easy." Dylan comes in every day by himself and it's real casual, and he basically keeps to himself. Once in a while he'll go hang out in the parking lot. One day I was heading out in my car and I see Dylan going out by himself but I don't stop. About a minute later I start thinking that I better go check on him so I turn my car around and start looking for him. I turn the corner and just as I see him people out on the street start recognizing him and are doing a "There's Bob Dylan, there's Bob Dylan" type of thing. Just then I pull up and he jumps in the car and we screech away. It was great timing!

**ST:** The Dead-Dylan collaboration worked out well.

RON DELANY

**DL:** The *Dylan and the Dead* album captures how they sounded.

**ST:** The Dead do quite a bit of Dylan's material at their own shows.

**DL:** I remember that when the Dead-Dylan collaboration seemed like a good possibility the band had me go out and buy as many Dylan CDs as I could so that they could familiarize themselves with his material. After that a lot of his material started to come into the repertoire.

TIM MOSENFELDER

## GABE HARRIS

Gabe Harris is the son of Joan Baez and David Harris. Since going to his first Dead concert at the Frost Amphitheatre at Stanford University in 1982 he has seen over fifty shows and is a confirmed Dead Head.

**ST:** What was it like growing up around musicians and political activists in terms of your outlook and viewpoints?

**GH:** When I was smaller I didn't really know what my parents were doing. I was at the age to become aware of what my parents had done and what their political significance was when I went to high school in Massachusetts. When I was at school I started finding out more about them because I was meeting people who were politically aware and I became more interested in politics myself.

**ST:** Tell me about your dad.

**GH:** He was a draft resister who spent twenty months in prison for resisting the draft. One of the books he's written is called *Mama I Should've Been Home Yesterday*. The subtitle was "20 Months In Prison For Not Killing Anybody," about his stay in prison. I read his book and it told me a few things about my dad I didn't know, and expanded my political views. Neither of my parents ever tried to force their politics on me and make it a part of my life. They let me figure it all out for myself. Now I'm amazed at the things they did.

**ST:** I understand that your mom was pregnant with you when she performed at Woodstock.

**GH:** Yes, I was born on December 2, 1969.

**ST:** What was it like growing up with all that great music your mom had to offer?

**GH:** I was always around it, obviously. When I was younger I wasn't too interested because I did not know what it was like to be without it. My mom sang me some wonderful lullabies though, and more recently I've become more involved with music. When I was younger I went on tour with my mom and at concerts I would run around backstage and explore the place. I never really checked out the music too much, until more recently.

**ST:** What was it like being around Bob Dylan?

**GH:** When I was younger I went on tour with him and my mother. I always liked him and thought he was a great guy but I never paid too much attention to his music. Now I listen to his music and I am amazed by the amount of songs he's written and what he has to say.

**ST:** How do you like how the Dead do Bob Dylan's songs?

**GH:** When I hear the Grateful Dead do his songs it's strange for me because I remember him from my childhood and I relate it to memories of my mom. She told me about the

RICK BRACKETT

first time she ever played with Dylan. If I remember correctly, he came out on stage during her tour and the crowd booed him off. She had to go out on stage and tell the crowd to give him a chance. It emphasizes to me how my mom is such a big part of this whole scene.

ST:  When did you get seriously interested in music?

GH:  I always liked to listen to different kinds of music but I never paid too much attention to it until my roommate in boarding school, who was a Dead Head, turned me on to listening to the Grateful Dead. I do remember that the first show I went to as a member of the audience was when I was twelve years old at the Frost Amphitheatre. I went with some friends of my mom's. I went to the backstage entrance and sent a note to Mickey Hart, who was a friend of my mom's. I had spent some time at his ranch. I like Mickey a lot. I sent a note to him and he came out and gave me a hug and brought me on stage and set me on this chest that was behind "The Beast." I sat there for the whole show and saw something I'd never seen before. It left a strong impression on me. I saw a lot of happy people in the audience, and watching Mickey drum was very intense.

ST:  How many Dead shows have you been to since that Frost show?

GH:  I would say at least fifty, all on the West Coast.

ST:  What is it about Grateful Dead music that makes it important to you?

GH:  Every time I go to a Grateful Dead show it's a healing event for me. It's a few days to let myself go, being in an environment where I feel comfortable doing whatever I want to do, listening to the music. Many of their songs have had an impact on me emotionally, and helped me grow. I love the music. The Dead are not afraid to try something new and interact with other musicians like Airto, Olatunji, or Clarence Clemons. I think Mickey's influence has a lot to do with it. I saw Planet Drum with Mickey, Airto, Olatunji, Hamza El-Din, and some other percussionists. It was amazing to see drummers from all over the world performing together. I love when the Dead do the rhythm devils portion of the show. The drums and space jams are usually incredible. One unique thing about the Grateful Dead is that each show is different.

ST:  In the '60s people expressed themselves more in their

behavior and also in their dress, but at Dead shows people behave and dress in a style more reminiscent of the '60s.

GH: I like to dress outrageously at shows. For instance, I've got these sunglasses that have feathers sticking out of them. I can be comfortable at a Dead show wearing them. Whenever I go to a show I want to do something to make other people laugh or smile. That's why I got the sunglasses. People walk around and do things like that. I want to contribute to the whole scene and make it more enjoyable for everyone. Dead Heads are a group of people that care about each other. At the Frost, some guy who worked at a bakery in Berkeley came by with his car loaded with bread and he gave it all away to people outside the show.

I remember going to Cal Expo in 1986 and it was an overcast day. I was walking around outside carrying my drum with me. These guys were making a big pot of stew out in back of their van. They called me over and I sat down and started playing my drum with them. Slowly people started coming around and bringing their own instruments and getting into it. This lady came up and said she could do an Indian Sun Dance if we had a rattlesnake rattle. I thought, geez, that's not real likely! The guy making the stew jumps up and says "I've got one in the van." He pulls one out and the lady starts shaking the rattle and doing her thing, and sure enough the sun came out.

ST: What kind of drum did you have?

GH: It came from Mickey Hart, actually. I remember Mickey, my mom, and I were walking around at the beach one day and he had this drum he was playing. Mickey gave it to my mom, and I ended up getting it from her. I bring the drum to a lot of shows and play it.

ST: That's great. A drum that Mickey Hart had has gone full circle.

GH: One of my favorite things at Dead concerts is outside the show when people get together and have a drum circle. Everybody starts playing drums together and people start gathering around and get into sync with each other.

ST: The Dead scene is unique in that way.

GH: I think that the Dead scene stands out more now than it did in the '60s because society has become more conservative. Following the '60s, people became tired of political activism. People my age didn't have anything to do with the political activism of the '60s, and therefore are not tired of political activism. My generation is starting to realize what's going on in America, and some are not apathetic. When the Grateful Dead and others do benefits they are helping raise people's awareness to certain issues that are important.

ST: It seems that younger Dead Heads like yourself are into the same philosophy as some of the older Dead Heads.

GH: I think that's true. There are a lot of similar political attitudes. In a way it's frustrating because the political climate now is not the same as the '60s, when politics were active and people were speaking out. I'd like to see more people speak their minds. It's something I think will happen in the nineties. I know a lot of people with strong political views who are concerned about what our government has turned into. Hopefully, people will get involved and change things.

ST: It's great to see that younger people want to get involved in these political and global issues. You come from a tradition of political activism.

GH: I would like to think that I will do something, and be able to convey what I think, and to inspire people to stand up for what they think. I don't think it's right that our government can ignore what's going on in this country like the homeless or the environment. For instance, the oil spill in Alaska. The ecology in Alaska has sustained incredible damage and the public has not really spoken out about it. We are all part of the ecological system and if you destroy one part of it, we all suffer.

ST: Dead Heads tend to be part of a subculture.

GH: When *In the Dark* came out, many people rushed in that didn't necessarily get into the deeper part of the scene at first, but with time that has begun to change, and the ones that aren't completely into it have started disappearing. I have a friend who had never been to a Dead show, who got turned on to the scene and kept going to shows and making new friends. Now the Grateful Dead scene is a good part of his life. People become close at the shows. For me, that's one thing that draws me back. Every time I go it's like visiting my second family. Seeing all the people is half of it for me. With the increasing number of Dead Heads, it makes it more important for people to work together on the cooperative scene. People should pick up after themselves, and have respect for the environment.

**ST:** Many of the songs the Dead do are from the '60s. How do the songs have relevance for you?

**GH:** I can't relate the same way as someone who heard the song when it first came out during the '60s in the midst of the times would, but I pick up on what the song is saying. For instance, "Dear Mr. Fantasy" is a song that has had a major effect on my life. I originally listened to Traffic's version of it but when I heard the Dead do it, it meant a lot to me.

**ST:** The Dead are a slice of America. Many of their songs came out of the America blues and folk tradition. Some of the songs are a throwback to the '60s folk music scene which your mom was a major part of.

**GH:** My mom hosted an AIDS Benefit at the Warfield Theatre that Jerry Garcia and Bob Weir played at. It was in December of 1987 and was called "Joan Baez and Friends." Jerry and Bob played together and then my mom came out and performed with them on several songs. It was great be-

JAY BLAKESBERG

Joan Baez & Friends

cause it was the first time I remember seeing her play with someone that I listen to regularly. It gave me a different perspective on my mom's music and it gave me more respect for her singing, seeing her do songs that I really like and she does not usually do. After the show we went out to dinner with all the performers and we all sat at one long table. I remember Jerry and Bob were there, and I was sitting at one end of the table and at the other end was Bob Weir. The majority of the people were pretty clean cut, and then I am sitting there with long hair, tie-dye, and earrings, and I see Bob Weir looking at me with a "Who's that guy, how did he get here" kind of expression on his face.

ST: Your mom and the Grateful Dead have done many benefits.

GH: I think it's great that they're involved. Personally I would hope that more Dead Heads get involved too. As far as I'm concerned, the more awareness and activity concerning the environment and political issues, the better. That is something I feel strongly about.

Yassou N'Dour, Joan Baez, Peter Gabriel, Tracy Chapman, & Bruce Springsteen

**ST:** Didn't you get involved with a New Year's broadcast?

**GH:** I was contacted to help do the MCing part of the show with Justin Kreutzmann for the 1987-88 New Year's broadcast. It was my first appearance on TV without my mom. It was funny because I came in early before the show and got some good seats near the stage. My job was to go on live TV and talk about the show before it started and during the intermission. I remember I was at the seats for the first set and when the band took a break I realized that I had to be in the press box, which was pretty far away. I had to wade through this sea of people and run to the press box. When I got there I was out of breath, and I had to grab the microphone and talk live on the air. We were supposed to interview people in the audience. This one guy looked pretty high, his pupils were as big as his eyeballs, and Justin said to him, "People come from all over the country to see the Dead, where did you come from?" The guy looks at us and says, "The parking lot."

## STEVE CORNELL

Steve Cornell is a younger generation Dead Head whom the Grateful Dead have taken under their wing. Cornell was in an accident when he was a child and has been in a wheelchair since that time. Lloyd Bove, who works with handicapped kids, arranged with Eileen Law to have Cornell meet Jerry Garcia. Dreams sometimes do come true and Cornell has been on cloud nine ever since, enjoying the ride.

**ST:** Steve, why don't you give me some background information about how you came to be a fan of the Grateful Dead.

**SC:** I'm nineteen years old and I've been a fan since 1984. I went to my first Grateful Dead show at the Civic Center in Philadelphia on April 20, 1984.

**ST:** How many shows have you seen since the first show?

**SC:** I guess I've seen about fifty Dead shows.

**ST:** I understand that you got to meet Jerry Garcia?

**SC:** Yeah! Kind of via a friend of a friend of a friend. It was pretty much a miracle. Back in 1986 — I was in the hospital. I was planning on seeing the Grateful Dead for New Year's but it didn't work out because of medical problems.

I missed that New Year's show and while I was in the hospital I met a lady named Lloyd Bove who came back to my room and saw some posters on my wall and realized I was a Dead Head. She said she had a friend in California who has been a Dead Head for a long time and asked me if I ever thought about meeting Jerry. I said, yeah, I've thought about it but there's no conceivable way of meeting Jerry. And she said she'd see what she could do. I left the hospital in January and Lloyd and I became good friends and talked on the phone. The band happened to be coming around for a winter tour in March at the Spectrum in Philadelphia and she worked out something for the 30th so I would have backstage passes. I was supposed to go backstage and meet Jerry then. But the night of the show it was inconceivable for me to go back and meet Jerry because the Spectrum wasn't really designed for handicapped people to get to the backstage area. There was no way for wheelchairs to get to the backstage area and there wasn't an elevator. There were no exits from the backstage area in case of a fire. I was bummed because it didn't work out. But then we talked to Dennis McNally, the publicist for the Grateful Dead, and the next day I went to the show and Dennis let me in the press box with some personalities from a local radio station. I sat there through the first set and during intermission I went backstage to meet Jerry. At this time my brother, Bob, and a good friend, Mike Coppa, carried me down the stairs and we went into a back room connected to Jerry's dressing room. Jerry walked in the room accompanied by his daughter, Annabelle. We sat down during intermission and talked for 15-20 minutes. It was a dream come true. When Jerry came in, he introduced himself and I shook his hand. He was a real gentleman.

**ST:** Since that time you've had other opportunities to see the band and go backstage?

**SC:** I was at the show on July 4, 1987 at Sullivan Stadium in Foxboro, Massachusetts and it was a total miracle. I was there for the show with my brother, Bob, who took me from the far back end of the stadium and brought me down on the field and pushed me through thousands of people, clear up to the wall separating the crowd from the stage area. There was an extended first set because the band was playing with Bob Dylan. Near the stage people were shoving and it was getting kind of crowded. People further back in the crowd weren't aware of somebody in a wheelchair up close so I was getting bumped all around. My brother, Bob, asked a security guard if he would allow me to get beyond the wall to get away from the crowd. The next thing you know I had five or six people grabbing on my wheelchair and boosting me up. When the first set was over, they brought me on the stage. Then they pushed me backstage where the band was and I met Bill Kreutzmann. That was really special because I had seen Bill earlier that day while I was getting crushed by the crowd. I was kind of depressed and had my head down and I looked up and Bill was drumming and he looked down at me and he smiled like, you poor sonofabitch, and I looked up at him and shook my head, like can you believe this, and the next thing you know I was up on stage. And then I was backstage and everybody was so nice and extended their hand in greeting.

**ST:** The Grateful Dead started in 1965 before you were even born. What is it about the Dead's music that attracts you to it?

**SC:** The Grateful Dead give you clues about life. Their music fits in with daily life and the band sings about things that help a person get through life. The whole thing about life is to be humble and to appreciate what you have and not really look for what you don't have. The band really gives you that perspective. They help you find knowledge. They help you relate to people and help people relate to you. In my opinion, I think the Grateful Dead experience is about looking more inward, to try and better yourself to be the kind of person you would want to meet.

**ST:** Lately the band has been talking about bettering the environment, and they have been doing benefits for the Rain Forest and Greenpeace, and things like that. I think that's pretty synonymous with what you're saying. In other words, let's preserve and appreciate what we've got now, before it's gone.

**SC:** I think that people should stop worrying so much about the financial aspects of life and they should think about their children, and their children's children. I think that nowadays some people are more worried about their financial problems and they don't give a darn about what they do to the earth. As long as they make money, they don't care. I think that the band is trying to get across to people that they should care because their children will have to live on this planet also, and to respect what you have, and not abuse it.

**ST:** A song like "Standing on the Moon" tries to give people a broader perspective and a more global view of this planet.

**SC:** I think "Standing on the Moon" has a lot of messages that apply to present-day attitudes in people. Where Jerry says, "hear the cries of Central America and El Salvador," he's trying to give people who are apathetic other ways to look at the world and give them a new window to look through, which is the opposite of that apathetic point of view where people feel that unless it affects them directly, they don't really care. It's like with the destruction of the rain forests, it's giving the point of view that says that even though something is thousands of miles away, it's still at your back door because we all live on the same planet and we must respect the planet or it will dry up and fade away. We have to appreciate what we have and not take it for granted.

BETTY BETTS

## HOWARD BETTS

Howard Betts is Vice Consul at the American Consulate in Tijuana. Betts is one of only 4,000 foreign service officers who work in the State Department. He works in the citizen services section of the Consulate helping Americans in trouble in Mexico. Betts is also a Dead Head who first saw the Dead at the Del Mar Fairgrounds in San Diego, California, on September 22, 1968 and has been going to Dead concerts since that time.

ST: How long have you been a fan of the Grateful Dead?

HB: I have been a fan for over twenty years. I first saw the Dead at the Autumnal Equinox on September 22, 1968 at the Del Mar Race Track. It was a great show — the Grateful Dead, Sons of Champlin, Quicksilver, Taj Mahal, Mother Earth, and others. The first time I heard the Grateful Dead was on FM radio and it was "Golden Road" off the first album. I've seen the band approximately fifty times since then. I'm what you call a Dead Head Diplomat.

ST: What is it about the Grateful Dead that makes you want to keep going back to see them?

HB: Good music for one, and integrity in that music. The Grateful Dead have never altered their music to fit with the trends of the times. They sound like the Grateful Dead have always sounded.

They are diplomats of music and they play American music. It's American beauty. It's the product of our culture, but they are also willing to bring influences from other parts of the world into their music. That kind of musical exploration by the band is tremendous. Yet Grateful Dead music remains very much American music despite all the influences they have absorbed. It is American in the finest sense. It's liberal, it's experimental, it's willing to go off in new directions, which is what I think America is about. American society offers us incredible freedom to experiment. Some people in our society are uncomfortable with freedom but it is a guarantee in our society. Not everybody thinks Abbie Hoffman was a great patriot, but to me he was, despite some problems he had, because he stood for freedom, for being able to say what he thought, for testing the boundaries of our society, and for questioning authority.

ST: What is it about the band that appeals to younger fans that are from an era far different than the '60s?

HB: The Grateful Dead appeal to a group of people who don't always accept everything that they're told to accept, who don't always do everything they're told to do. People who are bright and precocious, and don't always do well with authority figures. If there is a band that was not an authority figure it is the Grateful Dead. What I remember about the '60s was that you didn't have to follow the mainstream. The band continues in that direction of being willing to explore different possibilities. Dead Heads seem to be willing to explore other directions. The experimentalism of the '60s is what the Dead embody.

**ST:** What values of the '60s do you see surviving to the nineties?

**HB:** What is nice is that as people from the '60s have grown older, some have become doctors, lawyers, or diplomats and some still retain ethics from the '60s and are trying to make the world a better place. The social agenda of the '60s has been accomplished in that we have a generation of people that will question authority, who will not accept blindly what the government tells them. That is a massive difference for the politics of the future. A society that is willing to examine is a society that is strong; a society that is only willing to obey, is a society that is heading for trouble.

**ST:** How do you feel about the Grateful Dead taking on some of the global issues like the destruction of the rain forests?

**HB:** I work on environmental issues for the State Department and I'm extremely happy to see the band lending its good name and its efforts on behalf of an issue I see as being incredibly important. The rain forests are the lungs of our planet and if they are destroyed, our planet is in trouble. The band is getting out and helping a generation that is not as aware of environmental issues as people were in the '60s. The issue of planetary survival is very important and is another bus we can all get on. The more people realize that environmental issues are global issues, the better off the planet is going to be and the better off our children's future is going to be.

STEVE PERELSON

## TONY SERRA

Tony Serra is one of the most prominent criminal defense lawyers in the United States. Serra's been described as the counterculture's warrior lawyer. Serra is the model for the hippie attorney in the movie *True Believer* which stars James Woods. The movie is loosely based on Serra's successful defense of a Korean immigrant wrongfully convicted of murder after the conviction was set aside on appeal. After twenty years as a radical lawyer Serra operates well outside the American mainstream. A native San Franciscan, he has been going to Grateful Dead concerts since 1965.

**ST:** You were part of the '60s psychedelic music scene and went to the Fillmore Auditorium. What was it like?

**TS:** I went to a lot of them, and took to it like a duck to water. I was living above Haight-Ashbury when all of this broke out in the '60s. I was up the hill — within walking distance of Haight-Ashbury. I became a dance freak then because I was coming out of an athletic background. I had always done team sports. So, somehow, dancing to a frenzy every night was fabulous. It was a workout at a physical level with a spiritual flow and so, I became a dance freak. At least two or three nights a week I'd be going to the Fillmore or wherever else the music was happening.

At midnight they would have a price change and we would all wait for the price change. I remember we would go in our dumpy cars and we would bring an extra set of clothes, t-shirt, socks, because when we came out after dancing all night we had worked up a sweat and we would change clothes so we wouldn't catch a cold.

**ST:** What was Haight-Ashbury like in 1966?

**TS:** To see the flow of humanity that started in 1966 into Haight-Ashbury and flowing out to other areas in the Bay Area, it's unbelievable and like a dream, yet it was true. Every imaginable type of person, the richness of the cultural backgrounds, the ethnic conglomeration. Every form of human being was there, if you can imagine. Everything was music, art, smells, fragrances, lace, beads, acting out ... everything became a form of metaphor and allegory. The conventional would be street theater but it was all unconventional. It was all spontaneous human behavior. It's unprecedented in history.

It was interactive, peaceful, loving, holding hands. At one level, fleshy and sensuous. At another level, high and ethereal. It was unbelievable. You could spend hours walking up and down Haight-Ashbury, talking, looking, smiling, smelling, wondering, and laughing. What an era! Something is going on here. Something is definitely going on. Everyone knew that it was unprecedented and unparalleled, that it may never come again, that it was not going to last. It was like some rare growth that couldn't last for long. The oxygen that served it was rare. It attracted all walks of life.

**ST:** Did you go to the Trips Festival at Longshoremen's Hall in January of 1966?

**TS:** Yes, I went to that but I can only give you a merger of impressions from that whole era because it's hard for me to isolate specific concerts since I was at 80% of them. The first meaningful thing which goes on is that then, and even now at certain concerts, 90% of the people are under the influence of a drug. So start there. It's hard to explain to people who haven't experimented in psychedelic drugs what that means but it means things like seeing music, being engulfed in the physicality of sound, being immersed in the chromatic zone, entering into yellowness.

I haven't developed a vocabulary to describe those things but at one level it's chemical — you're seeing molecules and atoms, there's a molecular surface to reality, at another level there's fantasy. I'm just talking about one drug dimension, which I'll even call subjective from music, people, song, and from the event. But you're immersed in a sensorium and it's fused together. There's a reality, a perception that's keen and clairvoyant about people's psychological growth and the symbolism of their vocabulary, their expressions, so it's an interpersonal thing and then it gets larger than that because what's mixed into that are true hallucinations, for me always beautiful, your perception of existence, and then profound thought.

I was a philosophy major and it's like you've revisited, almost instinctually, all of the profound issues that philosophy has raised by the nature of existence, what's knowledge, what's life, what's death, and what's holy. All of this is just mixed into one experience as the concert is going and the wildness of the dance and you're shaking your head, your body is throbbing, and colors are flitting all over, and there's a sound like you're being immersed and you're being swept away, your psyche is being parted from your body, you're floating, and flashing. And this is the beginning of some new awareness. You return to a rhythm and you have a firmer grasp on reality. That's what made it completely different. That's why on flashbacks through groups like the Dead you relive all of those pristine experiences you had on psychedelics. Certainly everyone around was like that in various categories. People would be making love in front of you, other people were naked, oiling each other, and other people were dancing more wildly than anything you can imagine. You think you've seen the whole evolution of man portrayed symbolically, like groveling earth-types that look Neanderthal and all the way to ethereal elongated figures like post-El Greco forms that are spiritual, shadowy, sensuous, and have no real focus to them, they're like smoke.

Things become meaningful at a concert like, traditionally, looking into the heart of a flower and examining a ring or sparkle or facet of some type of jewelry, to grandiose visions, like sound emanating from the stage and you have visions of whatever salvation or you have notions of metaphysical pouring out at a distance, a fountain of light, a flowing type of feeling. Those experiences merge now almost as a single entity. In retrospect, you see all these fabulous images, some subjective, some fantasy, all emanating from reality. One of my strongest recollections is the beautiful, beautiful people like children, young adults, dogs, older people, all with beatific smiles, openness, goodness, the freshness of their consciousness. The banner was love, like everyone was truly in love with life's existence, with self, with goodness. It was mystic and turned to the East at one level, knowledge and wisdom.

It was a psychedelic kind of awareness that was rich and embroidered the fabric of the concerts. People addressed mysticism in their dances and some of them looked like belly dancers, others doing dances that looked like they were from Siam, some others middle-Eastern with capes and flowing gowns and scarves. I even saw a man and woman dressed in wolf skin who arrived on a motorcycle. It was overwhelming. An encounter never to be forgotten, so deep that it instills in your DNA for generations untold to come — the feeling of it — the overwhelming of it, and yet it was all positive, there was no negative. There were no bad trips on acid, none of that happened. I didn't see any of that and I was there the whole time.

You know, if you go into a room and you listen to enough people who have taken alcohol and there's another crowd that is just smoking grass, all the bad vibes come from the alcohol. Alcohol is related to aggression and there are statistics to show that. Psychedelics are related to peace, love, co-existence, harmony, aesthetics, and all of those things. And so it became, and still is for me, like a religion. It's like we, in a certain way, divest ourselves of our religious traditions and yet the nature of man needs something like that. For me, those concerts, as wild, sensual, and organic as they become, are a religious experience where people throw their mentality to unify their consciousness. They merge and throb as one thing. They center themselves and reach out and hold each other in their own form of spiritual embrace. And the music is like the pulpit. It's like where the truth is emanated from. It's the unifying factor. It's the fountain of wisdom, it's the channel to godliness, it's the purge and cleanse.

I'm a lawyer and lots of times I'm doing terribly tragic cases, and so I see a lot of pain and agony and yet I've never been let down by music. It always uplifts, it always frees, it shows the balance, the ultimate harmony of existence and so you're not brought down by stress and what other people call pain and suffering. You're not just tending lepers. The music has its own form of salvation to it so you keep going to the concerts and seeking those experiences and merging them with flashbacks and creating anew and always coming out in the present fresh and cleansed in terms of your emotional and spiritual perspective.

ST: Weren't the light shows an integral part of the experience?

TS: I miss the light shows. I remember the old rear projections with the liquid light. That was something! They were really reproducing acid vision and it was in your mind, it was up there. I remember there was Glen McCabe and Jerry Abrams, the two high priests of the light show. I'm sorry not to see that phenomenon as an art form still being explored and expanded. That part we lost. Somehow there should have been funding resources provided to keep that viable because those were art forms peculiar to the '60s that we've lost. They're extinct. They did it for a while in a museum. I remember a woman who worked with Glen McCabe that did liquid mirror projections in various museums of art, like an art form. After the Dead concerts she would go around doing it as an art phenomenon but she doesn't do it any more because she's dead. Few people remember it.

ST: The '60s posters seemed to recreate the experience. You could look at a poster and say, man, that's it! I don't know what it was, but they really captured the acid experience.

TS: Well, of course, you brought another high art form skill to this phenomenon. Here you had these artists coming out, many of them, and they were putting their energy into psychedelics, which was their creation and that's what it came out to be, just like the music came out to be.

ST: The Grateful Dead have been an integral part of the whole San Francisco psychedelic music scene and they are true survivors. Their new album is called *Built to Last* and, in fact, you mentioned that when you go to a Grateful Dead concert it's a timeless experience, like a deja vu experience. It opens a door. You close your eyes — it's the same music, the same kinds of people are there, and the same vibes are there. It opens a door and it's a timeless experience, like you are in an elevator shaft falling in darkness.

**TS:** That's completely true. The clothes, the attire, the eyes, the sensuality, the spiritual elements, all exactly as it was. The preservation of the colors, tie-dyes, dancing, and openness, which permits a person of my age to still go, gives you that timelessness that you spoke of. You go to touch that and to touch the religious aspect of it, to bathe in it, to be reborn or rejuvenated once again, but they've grown. They are not just rehashing their past or perpetuating some past vision. A lot of times you see a religion, like Christianity, you are perpetuating a vision. Christ was pretty heavy and his impact was large and for a long time, thousands of years, we've tried to perpetuate that vision in terms of passing the word and using metaphor. The Dead aren't doing that.

The Dead are still paving new paths. That's the beauty of them. But some of it I find in the category of rehearsing the past. I find that sentimental, romantic, nostalgic, beautiful, and uplifting. Some of the riffs are musical genius, obviously. I could get into that and that would be sufficient and that would last forever. But what they are doing is something much bigger than that. What I like most is about halfway through the second set where they'll get into what I'll call non-representational content, abstract sounds, space sounds, metaphysical sounds, and I like that most of all. That's open-ended. They are exploring there and that's going far out because of the technology and the skill, as any group has ever gone out. It's not the drugs in me that really respond to that. If there's something fundamental or futuristic about that part of every performance, that's why I'm there. You want live, spontaneous, active creation, instinctual imagination, or some kind of projected fantasy. I'm totally in awe, a lost pilgrim of metaphysical realms. They guide you where you need guidance. You are taking your consciousness and handing it over, and it's shattered, like a thousand feathers and it's floating there, little pieces of your mind, feelings, sensations, and understanding. And whatever crystallizes, explodes, and it carries back to some linear form and you remember where you are, who you are, and what you are.

They are still space traveling, on the hot lip of creation in terms of musical awareness. They're doing something that no one has done before. You get the feeling that you're going into areas with them, what I would call non-representational sound, metaphoric noise, cacophony which is open in harmony. You're traveling with them and going new ways and on new paths. That's what I like.

I enjoy the sentiment and the old familiar refrains; they bring tears to your eyes, you think about old places you've been, all the people you've known, and things you've done in instant flashback. I love that, and that would be enough, but the point to be made is why they're enduring, why they're vital, why they're significant, why they're growing, why greater honors are being bestowed on them. It's because they are still paving the future direction of music in those abstract sounds that they do so well and, from my point, technologically, they probably put more money into their equipment that produces those sounds and you're getting the acme of perfection in that area. That's what really draws my consciousness in. You can't stop it, it just flows with it.

**ST:** I was talking to Rock Scully, the Dead's former manager, and there's a consensus that the Frost is one of the favorite places for the band to play.

There is something about the simplicity of the Frost, the trees, the grass, it's like a throwback to a different era. You go in there and it's kind of like being in a pyramid chamber where you feel a oneness. You walk into that little oval meadow there, it's green, it's pretty, everyone is happy and it's a non-threatening environment. In this day and age with all the horror that life exposes, that venue is magical. You feel good. Maybe it's nostalgic because that's where the band started. Maybe it's a beautiful venue. Maybe it's all of those things. For whatever reason, it all comes together there. It's like a perfect string of pearls. The band feels relaxed and they don't feel any pressure. It's their home town. Everybody feels good and they all have a good time.

**TS:** I agree and can add a few other dimensions. Stanford is reputed to be one of the institutions of higher learning throughout the country, at least one of the top ten universities in our country. The welding together of music and pursuit of higher knowledge is an actual. That is, what we would always say in the early '60s, religion is dead and all of the music should move into the churches. In other words, the churches should vacate and allow the rock era to use these forums for a new form of religion. It didn't happen. In a few rare instances I've seen performances in grand cathedrals but it didn't supplant the next place.

Music loves a proper environment, an uplifting environment, and certainly a grand cathedral is that kind of environment. The next is higher institutions of education. It belongs there. It should be cradled there. It should have a sanctuary. It should be cloistered and pure and have no worry about police, traffic, or guns. It has to be a sanctuary within a sanctuary. Something that is pristine, beautiful, aesthetic, secure, and something that has a time-honored tradition of revering that type of an experience. That's why Stanford is metaphysically perfect for the event. It's renown as an educational center. That's where rare beautiful music belongs and then the spot that you talked about, that fabulously aesthetic environment there with beautiful weather, rolling hills, and eucalyptus trees, invites this type of pageantry.

ST:  The Grateful Dead recognize the audience is an important part of the experience. There's a symbiotic relationship between the band and the audience, and the better the time the audience is having, the better the band feels. The pageantry and whole experience of the Grateful Dead encompasses more than just the band. It's the whole experience.

TS:  Once again, I agree, and it has precedence in other levels. That is, for a long, long time people regarded art as something to look at. You would go into an art gallery and look at paintings and sculpture. When you went to a traditional musical event, you sat as a spectator and listened. So you were either looking or listening and there was no relationship between the performer and the spectator or audience. You were supposed to listen and see. That started to bring down a lot of art forms. In living sculpture, persons became part of the piece and were invited to react in terms of a piece. You would do a piece of sculpture and people would walk into it. It would be multi-dimensional. A sculpture would move, a sculpture could have odor, a sculpture could have sound, and the spectator's reaction to the sound was as meaningful to the total piece as was the sound itself. There wasn't this artificial distinction. If you will remember the very early '60s, going to plays in the lower East side of New York, the audience was an integral part. The audience would participate. There was no place to sit. When you went into the theater you were on the stage. You were part of the event. You were the event. With guidance from professional actors, it was open-ended. That came to music also. And so the relationship between the audience and the performers on stage was broken down. It is symbiotic or a mutuality of relationships; it's reciprocity, and it's the uniqueness of it. You realize that you're one of these little molecules of form. You're not isolated. You're not there on the outside. It's a difficult feeling. You go through something that's significant. It's humbling and belittling sometimes to think it's so grandiose and you are so insignificant. But if you become part of that, then it enhances everything, really. You probably reach your zenith in terms of conscious phenomenon at a Dead concert where everybody's dancing. From the minute it starts, you're up there dancing and getting wilder and wilder. And you look around and see behind the trees, in the trees, in the forest, everybody is dancing.

Outside the area, they're all dancing. Like it's instant combustion. And that is like an aura, a vibration, your metaphysical connection that makes the event higher and higher. No one has any inhibitions to express feeling or form, to respond, or reciprocate. You lose any notion of restraint, pride, or conventional inhibitors. The beauty of it is a free-flowing, unpredictable thing where you can almost direct it yourself. You're caught with energy.

ST:  I understand that you ran for Mayor of San Francisco.

TS:  Yes. That was in 1971; a Hippie party was created. Two persons ran for the Board of Supervisors and I ran for mayor. It was called the Platypus Party. We chose the platypus because it had evolved: change by evolution not revolution, that sort of thing. It had peacefully coexisted since prehistoric times. Like the image "We Will Survive" of the Dead, it had survived through peaceful coexistence and not through marauding, territorial expansion, exploitation, or any of the things the '60s was trying to make a statement against. It combined various adaptive features of a generic mammal, reptile, and duck. The platypus is a mixed metaphor. So you probably recall there were a lot of people, who, through psychedelics and music, believed we were mutations. The platypus connected with this higher level of awareness and peacefulness, which could be brought about by evolutionary mutation. Survival of the fittest.

We put it all together with the political platitudes of that day so we ran on a campaign called the Platypus Platform.

We had all of them, Platypus planning, Platypus positions, Platypus presents ... all this alliteration. We had a lot of veterans and proposed making San Francisco a sanctuary from the U.S. draft for the Vietnam War. "Make San Francisco a sanctuary against paying the IRS." I have been, and many at that time were, IRS resistors because of the war and the directions of politics. "Make San Francisco free from arrest for victimless crimes," i.e., obscenity, drugs, nudity, etc. We wanted to allegorically secede from the country and become a city-state like Athens or Carthage was before, run our own economy, throw capitalism out like the oil companies, etc., and have a large green center like they've done in many urban developments where the only cars permitted are those that run on batteries so there would be no smog, etc.

It wasn't for real but it was the notion of seizing a forum ... if you run, you get equal media time. So I ran as mayor. I got to make speeches. I received television and radio coverage and was invited to everything because they have to give you equal time. Eleven persons ran for mayor that year and, except for myself, they placed in direct relationship to their resources or funding. The winner was Alioto, who was miles ahead of everyone, and I came in 6th, which was right in the middle. Ahead of me were the real parties, the real spenders, and I beat the five symbolics which included the Communists, the Freedom and Speech Party. I did really good. I came right out in the middle.

We were grabbing a forum to speak the Platypus platitudes to the uninformed. You normally preach to the converted but we were saying these things in another way to reach people who hadn't really considered them or didn't consider them viable. It was fabulous and we did real well. I'm not really a business person and although we knew we couldn't possibly win, it was kind of like a win itself.

ST:   Didn't you have some bands who helped out?

TS:   Yes. We had several groups but the most prominent was Hot Tuna and they played free at a great number of functions. Music was part of politics then. The major events were political in those days. The groups were right there in the front position to be political and politicize the environment. I've been offered backstage passes for various groups like the Jefferson Airplane and the Dead through the years but I want to be out there dancing down front. So I've never required the intimacy of the "in" crowd. And, consequently, I'm speaking from being out there, dancing wildly.

ST: What is it about the Grateful Dead that has made them endure and have such significance to so many people, for so long, and for a new generation of people?

TS: You'd have to know the Dead. Here's what I would infer:
(1) They have sacrificed a lot of their personal needs and gratifications in order to stay united to give good music and allow their art to flourish, subordinating their personal needs. I think you have to do that as great artists and they've done that. And that means having nothing of greater priority. Nothing of greater priority than their music. Family is secondary. Certainly all economics and health are also secondary to the music. That's like your contribution.
(2) I guess it is the self-identification that you are necessary to preserve a historical phenomenon, like you're the seed carrier, you're the bearer of the words so to speak, and if you go, maybe it will all go. It's bigger than you. You have to give yourself to it. The formula that produced you is greater than you ... you must serve that formula. There's too much of a need. You are too embroiled. It's that kind of sacrifice.
(3) They're good and have genius and skills and imagination, and are still creating. They persevere.
(4) The last thing that really makes them is the movement that supports them. There are people out there that believe in the psychedelic awareness, the collective unity of consciousness. The people that believe in those kinds of things identify the Dead as some kind of a guide in life, and that kind of following buoys anyone up. It gives strength to any phenomenon.

So it's certainly a combination of factors of why they exist and why they have lasted. It's not just because they are genius and their music is still evolving because there's lots of phenomena that have that. It takes these other types of stabilizing factors, but whatever it is let's just hope it continues.

Vince Welnick & Bruce Hornsby
Playing in the Band — Europe '90.

*TOP* — Double Exposure of the
Grateful Dead and the Liberated
Brandenburg Gate-Berlin '90.

The Music Never Stopped....                    275

DEBRA TROY

RUE GUISARDE, PARIS, '90

# ONE MORE SATURDAY NIGHT

Full color T-shirts & Posters are
available by mail order.
Send a money order in the amount of
$12.50 for a poster or $17.50 for
a T-shirt (M, L & XL)

## to:

## MOUSE & COMPANY

P.O. Box 302016
Escondido, CA 92030

Price includes Postage & Handling.